Good old days,
Alibis and
Outright Lies

Good Old Guys Alibis and Outright Lies

Bob Scammell

Blue Ribbon Books

Johnson Gorman Publishers

The Publishers
Johnson Gorman Publishers
3669 — 41 Avenue
Red Deer Alberta Canada T4N 2X7

Credits
Cover art and text illustrations by David Soltess.
Design by Full Court Press Inc.
Printed & Bound in Canada by Webcom Limited for Johnson
Gorman Publishers.

Acknowledgements
Financial support provided by the Alberta Foundation for the
Arts, a beneficiary of the Lottery Fund of the Government of
Alberta.

COMMITTED TO THE DEVELOPMENT OF CULTURE AND THE ARTS

Canadian Cataloguing in Publication Data
Scammell, Bob, 1937–
Good old guys, alibis and outright lies
ISBN 0—921835—19—1
1. Fishing–Humor. 2. Hunting–Humor. 3. Outdoor life–
Humor. I. Title. II. Series.
SK33.S27   1996   799'.0207   C96-910651-3

Author's Acknowledgments

The majority of the pieces collected here were first published in *The Outdoor Edge*, to which I am grateful for the permission to reprint and for the help of editor and friend Ken Bailey in developing my regular humor column, "Just for Laughs." Other thanks go to the following publications, where the named pieces first saw print, sometimes in slightly different form: *The Alberta Fishing Guide* for "How I Started the Guv Fishing Again and Went to Hell, Maybe," "I and the Egg" and "Hard Water Porn"; *Western Sportsman* for "Pheasant Fillosopher"; *Alberta's Hunting & Fishing Magazine* for "Gunner's Alibi"; the various newspapers in which my weekly column has appeared, particularly the *Red Deer Advocate*, the *Brooks Bulletin* and the *Rocky Mountain House Mountaineer* for "Hunting the Moggie" and "The Where-to of How-to"; the *Alberta Hunting Guide* for "Miracle Moose and Mal Demise"; and *Outdoor Canada* for "Getting Found Out." Finally, Greg Norman and Trout Unlimited in whose book *Fish and Tell and Go to Hell* "Vested Interests" first appeared in a longer and different version.

Contents

Tracking Laughter: An Introduction

MY FIRST OUTDOORS PUBLISHER, the late Patrick J. O'Callaghan, then of the *Red Deer Advocate*, taught me an important lesson. I had done one of my early pieces of humor, satire even, and a reader took it seriously, was outraged and raised hell with the boss.

"You have to remember," Pat told me, "no laugh track, no dubbed laughter comes with the written word to tell serious people when you aren't being serious, so they may laugh."

Perhaps, the boss suggested, we should label my funny stuff "Laugh if It Feels Right" or "Beware, Satire Ahead." Good idea, particularly with outdoors humor, which comes in many forms. So, the label, the title: *Good Old Guys, Alibis and Outright Lies*. Tall tales, excuses, alibis and outright lies are frequent whenever outdoors people are trading truths, and thus they are frequent components of much outdoors writing. (Incidentally, I would have much preferred *Damned Lies* to *Outright*, but I also learned a long time ago that most editors of media that publish outdoors stuff are convinced outdoors people are all patriotic and God fearing, never use profanity or have lewd thoughts and never permit writers to suggest otherwise. Obviously editors hang out with a different species of outdoors person than the rest of us do.)

Outdoors humorists run the gamut from the super sophisticated word play of the late, zany Ed Zern to the folksy hilarity of Patrick J. McManus, featuring vivid sight gags in prose and unforgettable one-liners. A rare form of outdoors humor is the parody. Somehow I suspect Zern and McManus are impossible to parody, but I fear I will have to try some day.

There is no way I could resist a parody, a spoof, of the

deadly serious, unique style of fly-fishing guru and voluminous writer Ernest Schwiebert, who is an accidental humorist. "I and the Egg: Caviar Emptor, Ernie," brought me one of the more useful (it is giving me a line here) and hilarious rejection slips I have ever received, from Dennis Bitton, then the deadly serious editor of *The Flyfisher,* published by the Federation of Fly Fishers. It read: "While it's an intriguing fly, I don't think I want to promote something that could foul hook so easily."

Was Bitton thinking I was seriously advocating the "Ha-Ha Fly," or was he actually telling me, "Really! We can't mock the gods of the fly-fishing industry, can we?"

Here I have to digress, as have many writers of humor, to say that you cannot make up anything sufficiently ridiculous that modern civilization will not out-gross, as the kids say, within a week. Shortly after "I and the Egg" was published, my now-deceased old friend Charlie Brooks seriously claimed in his book *Henry's Fork* to have seen trout feeding selectively on salmon fly eggs one day. In early drafts of "Serious What-tail Bizness" I agonized over telling the outrageous lie that human urine attracts deer. Then came the investigative reporting on the burgeoning scents industry and the flat assertion by some experts that human male urine is a better deer attractant than whatever it really is in some of those little squeeze bottles that the snake . . . er . . . deer oil salesmen sell for more money per ounce than single malt Scotch.

Humor is subjective and will not be published unless the editor laughs. If he thinks a piece is funny, he is sure everyone else will, and verse vica. Thus, there are few writers who try humor on purpose, particularly outdoors writers. No outdoors humorist I have ever met, including McManus and Zern, even laughs at his own stuff. How could anyone else laugh? An editor? Don't make us laugh! Besides, there is little money in it unless you are a Zern or McManus. The Outdoor Writers of

America does hold a contest for its members for their published humor, but it is one of their few contests that has no sponsor and no handsome prizes in cash or in kind.

Readers have to understand that humorists seldom hate what they write about. I have a high regard for Ernie Schwiebert, respect for what he knows and what he has done for fly-fishing. I own almost every book he has written, but I also know that, like most angling gods, despite his huge ego, he rolls his waders down to a . . . ah . . . go in the bush, same as the rest of us.

There will be as many responses to humor pieces as there are readers, divided by their personal forms of brain damage. When a shorter version of "Hunting the Moggie" was published, some anonymous reader tore it out and mailed it back to me with "Sick, Sick" scrawled across it in black grease pencil. I cherish that trophy and may even be able to afford to have it framed some day. But that same reader would probably go all marshmallow-minded and misty-eyed over "It's Fishing—Cats and Dogs!" unless, of course, that person is of the inhuman group that believes it is cruelty to take a dog hunting, God forbid let a cat come fishing and eat anything but vegetables. Men laugh themselves silly over "How to Eschew Snoose"; women do not understand it. Of course, I have known women who are outdoors lovers and do a lot of other neat things, but only two have I even suspected of doing snoose.

You simply cannot be that herd bull of all oxymorons, politically correct, and write humor. If you are among the practitioners, your feelings might be hurt that some of these pieces seem to be saying ice fishing and moose hunting are antisocial afflictions, akin to our most fashionable forms of substance abuse. There, there; if I really put my mind to it, I am certain I could think of something negative to say about these perversions.

Like all outdoors humorists, I am a participant in favorite outdoors diversions of my own. I have been a constant reader of the "big three" outdoors magazines since I was knee high to a tackle box and am wounded to see them today slipping ever further into formula stories and no-brainer how-to stories like "The Where-to of How-to." Personally, too, I am hopelessly addicted to fly-fishing and pheasant hunting, and demented over my newest girlfriend, deer hunting, but still I worry about you other people who are far too serious about such things, particularly your own pet perversions. We must never forget that no matter how innocent the diversion, it leads to its own perversion as fast as the various outdoors industries can get it there.

We are all different. We all have some things that make us laugh and others that make us mad. But the most important message in this book is that outdoors people are far too serious about things that other people (who have only their own word to prove that they, themselves, are sane) find ridiculous.

What we all need is a little of that simplistic how-to: "How to Track Laughter," or "How to Dub Your Own." Feel free; be my guest, but beware that satire.

Good
Old
Guys

1

How I Started the Guv Fishing Again and Went to Hell, Maybe

IT MAY NOT BE POLITICALLY CORRECT TO NOTICE, BUT SOME immigrants will take on instant airs. My father, the Guv, got very uppity about fishing shortly after arriving in Canada from England, where all he could hunt was "moggies," which is what they called alley cats, and the best fishing he could do was "guddle" for the bar of soap in his Saturday night bath. He went first to the southwest interior of British Columbia and immediately got spoiled by snaking trout on a cast of wet flies, three at a time, out of virgin trout streams, smartly onto a logging camp supper table.

Unfortunately for me, I was not born yet because my father's B.C. experiences had ruined him for the fishing available where we lived after I came along: pike, walleyes, goldeyes, etcetera, in the vicinity of Brooks in southeastern Alberta. These creatures enthralled me, but the Guv regarded them as no better than the tench, gudgeon, dace and that ilk, the "course fish" that the common man could fish for in England.

The Guv just would not go fishing except for the annual week-long trout fishing forays during the war to the Pincher Creek area in southwestern Alberta, with his friends, to which small boys were not invited. The next morning after his scheduled late-night returns from these trips, I would rise early, open the fridge and go walleyed in its light at the color and the sweet smell of what I now know were the cutthroats, rainbows and bull trout lying in state, like so many Lenins in a tomb. It got me squirming and yearning, and not just to carry on to the bathroom. It was hunger, an unbearable hunger to go fishing, for any fish at all, anything—a hunger that would gnaw at me all my life. My fishing for the time being would be confined by the range of my bike. It was obvious I had to get the Guv fishing again if some of my own far-flung dreams were to be realized.

It has always seemed fitting to me that a pharmacist should have filled the prescription that cured my dad. Clark Masters was a positive inspiration to small boys; in fact he had inspired two fine ones of his own, who were grown, home from the war and busy getting their lives back together. Perhaps Mr. Masters was lonely for another small boy to inspire. Whatever the reason, Mr. Masters was convenient, living just down the lane from our house, when I heard the incredible rumor that he had been catching trout somewhere in the immediate vicinity.

Sometimes I wish I could be that shameless today; then I knew no better. I cornered him in his garden at home or in his dispensary downtown, but no matter what tricks and stratagems I employed, he would confess only that he had been catching trout, big ones, but would not tell me where. Finally, after playing me so long I now suspect he feared I would get off the hook, Mr. Masters said he would not tell me, but he would show me if I cared to accompany him and his wife, Alma, so fine and gentle a lady I was thunderstruck to learn she liked fishing, on Wednesday afternoon. Back then, in those golden old days, even drugstores closed on Sundays and Wednesday afternoons. Permission was readily granted by the Guv without even token reference to higher authority, my nonfishing mother.

Neither I nor my father had the slightest idea where I would be taken. En route, mileages and turns were memorized as though I were being kidnapped. We eventually arrived at a place I had heard about but never seen, the Antelope Creek Siphon. This was the place where the main canal bringing water from the Bassano Dam on the Bow River to Lake Newell, the main reservoir for the Eastern Irrigation District, must somehow get all that water through or over a deep and wide valley. The solution was two pipes, four to six feet in diameter, hugging the valley floor, operating like an upside down siphon. Water boiled and surged out the downstream ends of those pipes, then sighed, like my Nana getting out of her girdle, expanded and smoothed into a canal again. On each side, reached by a catwalk behind the gates, were low cement walls and a backwater where the surge first widened. In more recent years the Bow River, source of all that water, has become known as a world-class trout stream. Somehow, someone found that in those two backwaters on the bald-headed prairie, miles from the Bow, trout could be taken by an angler lolling on the wall and allowing a worm on a hook and one split shot to swirl around and around.

The Masters and I lazed on those warm cement walls in the bright sunshine and fished the afternoon away. As luck would tritely have it, the beginner had the *only* luck, two thirteen-inch rainbows, one from the backwater on each side. The length is branded on my brain because I recall thinking how appropriate it was that a thirteen-year-old's first trout should be thirteen inches. Also vivid is the memory of how excited Mr. Masters got when I hooked each of those fish and what he said he would do to me if I lost either. Something was also said on the ride home about the implications and consequences of revealing, ever, to anyone, where those trout were caught. That aspect merely reinforced what my own father had already passed on to me about the traditions of secrecy in angling, a tradition which, although I did not know it then and there in Mr. Master's car, was soon to be severely tried and tested.

For the first time ever I was responsible for trout lying in state in our fridge, and it was the Guv cracking the door, then sniffing that sweet smell. Walleyed? His eyes popped like button mushrooms; you could have brushed them off with a feather duster. His hands shook. Rumors of fishing holes, like rumors of war, are one thing: it is quite another when somebody produces a *corpus delicti*. Without pause, without taking his eyes from those fish, the Guv ground out the question nobody ever asks and nobody can ever resist asking.

"Where'd you get them?"

"Mr. Masters said not to tell."

Silence struck our kitchen. Then my father's expression darkened as he slammed the fridge door, dousing the light that had shone on his face. He whirled and left the house, slamming another door. I peeked at my mother. Her mouth was pursed, drawn by the opposing tugs on her heartstrings.

"Your own father . . . " she said.

"You never tell anyone. Dad knows I'm right."

How many days did my dad not speak to me? For me it was an eternity of agony; for my mom it was worse. She suggested I speak to Mr. Masters. I refused without explaining that by then I was terrified that not only would Mr. Masters absolve me by saying he had not meant my father, but he would also ventilate his legendary temper on me for being an impertinent and obnoxious young pup, disobedient and rude to my dad. Mr. Masters was of an older school than even the Guv, and in those days all citizens regarded the proper upbringing of the young, anybody's, as a sacred personal obligation.

Eventually Mother intervened. She told me she had discussed the situation with Mr. Masters on the phone and he said, of course I could tell my dad, but nobody else. That last part convinced me Mr. Masters could have said that because Mother never did understand enough about fishing, fishermen and their sacred oath of secrecy to make it up. From my mother I extracted the solemn promise she would never tell the Guv that Mr. Masters had authorized the leaking of the secret.

"Why?" she asked.

"Anyone who's not a father and doesn't fish wouldn't understand," I said, unfeelingly, "but it has to do with feelings."

"Oh!" she said. If there was one thing my mother thought she understood, it was feelings.

So I told all and insisted that it was my own decision and that I personally would take the consequences.

"Hmmm," the Guv mused. "Sure . . . it had to be Antelope Creek. Must be getting in there from the Bow."

Then he forgot trout and water, and returned suddenly to the real world. My dad shook my hand, as he always did in serious moments, then grinned and ruffled my hair.

On Saturday morning, a week after I got those trout (Mr. Masters could never leave the drugstore on Saturday), I received the first of what were to be many similar mid-Saturday morning calls from the Guv's office, calls that continued until the day when I no longer lived at home in the summers.

"Why don't you dig some worms," the Guv would suggest, "and get the gear ready. Ask Mom to make a lunch. I can get there about eleven."

There began the kind of fruitful father–son angling collaboration about which stories are written that mist the eyes, make it hard to swallow—stories which may even hold a grain of truth, but which were really hilarious, mostly, and which lasted for more than twenty-five years until the Guv died.

Gone were the Guv's delusions of grandeur. Over the years we fished together for virtually anything that swims in Alberta, sometimes even trout. Obviously the proximate possibility of trout and my willingness to breach the sacred anglers' covenant of secrecy convinced my father how important fishing of any kind was to me and should be to him.

The only aspect that has bothered me throughout the years has been to wonder whether Mom really did talk to Mr. Masters. Did I really get the Guv fishing again through a betrayal of the most sacred anglers' oath? Did Mr. Masters go through the rest of his life believing me to be a loose-lipped, low-down, fish-and-tell-and-go-to-hell angler? I'll never know, and I never dared ask. One thing is sure: either Mother's story was true and she did get the authorization from Mr. Masters or Mr. Masters never even knew his trust had been betrayed. Mom was known to white lie in a good cause—feelings, after all—and, as I have already said, the Guv was of the old school: he never told anyone, not even Mr. Masters, that he was catching any trout, let alone where.

2

My Outdoors Career

ONE DAY RECENTLY I RAN ACROSS BOTH A PAMPHLET AND A magazine article dealing with a "career in the outdoors," promoting the dream of all men to make their living doing what they love most: absolutely nothing.

That was the dream of many of us in my little hometown, but there were fewer options and variations than today. Back then, the primordial fish or wildlife biologist had not even evolved from the ooze and slime, let alone crawled back into it, where his species has toiled ever since. As envied role models we had only the odd game warden and, best of all, those odder, carefree vagabonds who did nothing all day but chase and band waterfowl for Ducks Unlimited and shoot snooker all night.

"Hmpfh," my mom would snort, "nothing but lazy, good-for-nothing dreamers, beer-swilling, tobacco-chewing, pool hall bums."

Mom may even have said something negative about our heroes, but nothing sufficient to disturb my career dreams.

In those days most of us were rich in only one thing: just across the street was all outdoors in which to train for our careers. There were swamps, sloughs, bluffs, canals, swales, tules, even orchards, and acres of plain, bald-headed prairie,

complete with all the furred, feathered, scaled and slimed creatures that dwell therein and thereon.

One of the first environmental battles I can remember was
when the town decided to fell the stately cottonwoods, the
boughs of which roofed our street, forming a sylvan tunnel
and the roots of which plugged sewer lines, turning every basement into muskeg. My father even wrote a poem, published in
our weekly newspaper, rhyming and defaming every one of the
guilty town councillors.

But the ancient cottonwoods came crashing down anyway.
Eventually their stumps turned punky and provided living lab-
oratories for the study of millions of insects. With a magnifying glass and associates who must remain nameless to this day,
I spied on the private lives of ants, beetles, etcetera. Later,
under intense cross-examination, I admitted that the smoldering of those stumps must have been the accidental and spon-
taneous result of the pure solar energy concentrated by our
lenses as we tracked those bugs.

After all, how could I admit the truth? In those days kids
attended Sunday school, period, and had to sing "God Sees the
Little Sparrow Fall." (Only some of us changed the second line
to: "Because He shoots a Daisy, too.") Thus we bore the guilt
of crimes too horrendous to admit. Did He not also hear the
howls of glee as we wretched urchins saw the little ant vapor-
ize into a puff of pungent formic acid or the cheers as Four
Eyes Feehan got a double on barbecued beetles with his thick
wire rims?

Several of the stumps started smoldering, then their punky
roots became long, slow fuses down into sewer lines and basements. Medicine Hat, seventy miles downwind, is proud that
Kipling, no less, called the place "the city with all hell for a
basement." For two weeks our town wore the pall of smoke to
prove in whose basements the fires of hell really smoldered.

Unfortunately one of the basements worst afflicted was just across the street from us, that of Charles Horatio Armand Powlett, the dean of our town's three lawyers. My alibi survived just one of C.H.'s three crafty questions, and then I was summarily dismissed, much impressed, for the first time, with a possible calling other than that of the wild.

My old man was not so lucky. Much later he emerged, shaken and ashen, from the remainder of the interview with C.H. My father confiscated my magnifying glass, thus delaying my entomological studies for a day or two. For the first time, too, I was made aware that lawyers were not among my old man's favorite people.

Diz, son of one of the town's other lawyers, was my first outdoors buddy. Diz possessed wonders beyond the means of any other kid in town: a three-speed bike, the first spinning reel ever seen by anyone from there to the correction line and an air pistol, believe it or not—all things that also got me thinking about careers and the ill-gotten gains thereof.

Diz's mother was a blithe spirit who would throw cocktail parties and cast pearls of the finest Beluga caviar before the swine of the town, such as my old man.

My father: "I'm not going to eat something that looks like bird shot and tastes like bird sh. . . ."

My mother: "Shhhh!"

The mornings after, without feeling disloyal, I would help Diz gobble all the leftover little squares of birdshot toast while Diz's mom, delighted, would recite poetry:

Caviar comes from the virgin sturgeon,
And the virgin sturgeon needs no urgin',
That's why caviar's a very rare dish.

Then she would hand me the whole Beluga can, worth probably a grand at today's prices, and a spoon, so I could finish it off like it was mere blackberry jam, or even ordinary

off-color tapioca. She would watch me, eyes dancing, and pro-
nounce, "Oh, you'll go a long way kid."

But first I went just as far as the Red Deer River, from
which I returned with two sturgeon, so forbidden in those days
that they were known as the "King's fish." My outraged royalist
old man decided that instead of turning me in he'd teach me a
lesson by making me clean, skin and eat them. But my sturgeon
were not virgins—at least they contained not one BB of caviar.
They were rich and delicious, however; mother and I smacked
our lips over the forbidden flesh while the old man sat there
munching cheese and crackers and huffing and puffing crumbs.

Diz and his dad were generous, too, and gave me lots of
good stuff. One day they turned up swaddled in seeping ban-
dages with a young, full-fledged Swainson's Hawk that they
dared not release from its straitjacket of gunny sacks. The
hawk and its frantic mother had torn them to shreds during
the hawk napping. I reared the bird and taught him to hunt.

I had nothing to do with the fact that my hawk, Satan,
hated human females. He may have learned it across the back
alley from Mr. Gresl's parrot, who was famous in our town for
being the world's first male chauvinist bird. In turn, I hated the
parrot for his perfect imitation of my mother calling me, she
whose calls had to be obeyed immediately. I admit I did get a
great paper route when our paper girl resigned the first time
she set foot onto our block when Satan was loose.

I suspect my hawk may have eaten Mrs. Newby's cat,
Muffy, who was in the habit of entertaining her gentlemen
friends in her brothel high in the boughs of a spruce tree that
always seemed to be quivering and yowling in feline ecstasy.
Muffy would lose her habitual wariness while thus engaged,
paying no heed whatever even of her mistress, who would
stand below the shivering, screaming spruce, crooning a coun-
terpoint of "come Muffy, come down, dear."

That case was not proven, but I was guilty on circumstantial evidence when I removed the leather jesses from the hawk's legs in September and, instead of flying south with others of his kind, Satan perched on the Powlett's front porch rail, where he spread his six-foot span, hissed, screamed and would not allow any woman or girl into the yard or out of the house.

This time my father emerged from Mr. Powlett's office totally stricken and asserting that, in reconsidering my career in the outdoors, I should also remember that, if I even thought of becoming a lawyer, he would disinherit me, all of which really got me thinking, as non-negotiable ultimatums always do with kids.

Actually I had been considering a career in medicine since I specialized in trouble anyway, but decided I favored the kind that did not involve blood, guts and bad smells.

In my high school graduating year Ms. (as she would be called now) Harridan, a school teacher, retired and gone to the hog heaven of a pig farm, who had recently been convicted of smuggling a Lincoln in from Nebraska, accosted me on the street.

"What are you going to do when you graduate?" she demanded.

"Study law," I announced, emerging from the closet for the first time.

"Hmpfh," she snorted, "lawyers are a dime a dozen."

"Not good ones who can beat smuggling charges," I retorted.

Ms. Harridan gleefully reported this conversation to my mother, who was so pleased that I was going to do something, anything, so long as it was indoors that she overlooked my rudeness to an old lady and forgot the hazards of being the messenger of bad news to my dad.

But my father set aside his personal antipathy to lawyers

and revealed his kindly tolerance of the ambitions of his only son. Inside or outside was of no concern to my old man, just so long as either was away. "He can't article with a local lawyer, can he?" he asked. "He has to leave home, at least as far as Edmonton, doesn't he?"

Turns out everyone was right but me. In thirty years of practicing matrimonial law I have endured more blood, guts and bad smells than an emergency medical response team. Oh, all outdoors is still there, and I do get out into it for a breath of fresh air once in a while, but I do it for love, not money, of which I have yet to save sufficient to eat Beluga caviar straight from the can just one more time.

3

Paying those Huntin' Uncle Dooz

BEFORE OUTDOORS EDUCATION, EVEN, LET ALONE THE Canadian Firearms Safety Course, beginners were "brung up right" in the outdoors pursuits by apprenticeship. You learned outdoors stuff from your father in the good old days, or from various replacement "huntin' uncles" if dad had lit out to hunt and fish fields and streams in the great beyond or, worse, did not hunt or fish anywhere.

First you whined and pestered to go, then the Articles of Apprenticeship were laid down: "Any of your whinin', complainin' or snivelin' out there, and you'll never go again, and don't tell Mom everything that goes on out there. Correction, don't tell Mom anything."

Anything and everything does happen, of course, while hunting and fishing—much of it gross, insufferable, uncomfortable, terrifying, even dangerous. There may even be some bad parts. Those little stoics with the good genes for toleration of misery eventually become master hunters and fishers; those that don't beller and bawl, tell mom all, then become something else altogether, maybe even amount to something like computer nerds or concert violinists, whatever.

The greatest living pool of outdoors genes I have ever known was Iain, son of Mac, a frequent hunting buddy, who came with us from the time he could walk. The only time I ever heard any bawling was the day the kid lost the fish bag with his dad's beer in it up on Elk Creek. Working in shifts, it only took an hour or so for Iain and me to comfort his dad and stop his sobs.

Many times in the rig on the way home Iain was delirious with exhaustion and could not be shut up, which was great, because babbling seemed to run him down so he had nothing left to tell his mom. So he kept on coming, aided also by the fact his dad is of the old school and broke down various teachers by excusing his son's absence on a pheasant trip with "a boy's education is too important to be frittered away in school."

My own dad, the Guv, was on some of those pheasant trips and often, late in the day, he would suggest to Iain that the "old guys" go back to the rig where there were cookies, chocolate bars and pop for the kid and his beloved Rocket Fuel hospital brandy for the Guv. Apparently the Guv would tell stories of the good old days and respond patiently to the lad's interminable questions and "but what if it dids" and "wuff it didn'ts."

Obviously my own old guy had mellowed. There were few cookies, chocolate bars and less sympathy during my apprenticeship to my dad. What there were in abundance were layered britches on me, the outermost pair generally being what are still called tin pants because they are alleged to be impervious to thistles, thorns, brambles and burrs. But my lips were sealed, mostly by the dried blood from facial lacerations and head wounds. Eventually Mom noted the bills tolling in for new tin pants to replace the pairs thorn-torn to mattress ticking. But the Guv convinced her it was one thing to have a valuable Labrador like old Buster cut up flushing, but quite another to have him torn to shreds retrieving birds out of those bullberry bluffs and wild rose jungles.

"The kid's got to share the load," the Guv told mom, "pay his dues."

The Guv taught me proper gun handling in the field by confiscating my ammunition and making me hunt with an empty shotgun all day, immediately spotting my slightest infraction of his rules of firearms safety. I swear I was eighteen the last time it happened. It was also the occasion of the only double I can remember ever doing on pheasants. I had them both gunned down, dead and half field-dressed before the Guv even got thumb to safety. He confiscated my remaining shells.

"What'd I do wrong?" I whined.

"You shot too fast."

Recently I took and passed that Canadian Firearms Safety Course, and I cannot recall in the "Vital Four" rules of firearms safety or the "Three Keys," anything against downing a double on roosters before dad gets his gun up.

We did not hunt big game because the Guv had burnt out on it his first winter in British Columbia when he had to kill deer to live. So Griz and I apprenticed to a huntin' uncle, a journeyman poacher who lived in little floored-over basement on the prairie.

Mom snorted, "Third-rate, worthless, smelly old bum."

She was wrong. He was first class in all of the above.

For our first deer hunt he drove us down to the mouth of a big coulee on the Red Deer River, outfitted us with overalls topped with tin pants and told us to hunt as quietly and slowly as we could up the coulee. He assured us as he rattled away in his old pickup that he would be up at the head of the coulee three miles away and would come down and help if he heard us shoot. But about half an hour after we got started, we heard a shot from up there. Down in the bottom, 200 hard yards from the rim at the coulee head was our mentor admiring a mule deer with a monstrous rack.

"Now ahm going to learn youse gutting my way," he said, handing Griz a knife and pointing at the big buck's belly.

"But where?" I started.

"Gutz'r in thar, boys, gittem out. Gotta pay yer dues."

Bitter, bloody but unbowed, Griz at one point looked up and said, "I always thought you were supposed to hunt deer upwind."

"Ah wuz," our huntin' uncle replied. "Gotta pay yer dues, boys. . . . But you done fine, just fine. It wasn't so much the scent, er even the snappin' of the bush as the quakin' of the earth that finally got them deers movin'."

When Griz and I finished up, our huntin' uncle peered up toward the coulee rimrock, 200 near-vertical yards above us.

"Now," he said, "Ahm goin' to learn you how come you never shoot no critter down in no hole like this. . . ."

"Gotta pay yer dues, boys," we all chimed in.

Forever after we called him Uncle Dooz. With fullest credit and apologies, he was to Patrick McManus's mentor, Rancid Crabtree, and as attractive as your sun-ripened dead cow is to a merely fragrant coyote. Uncle Dooz's teachings, nonteachings and outdoors gleanings would fill volumes, not to mention sanitary landfills. But it was all rare stuff not available from our stuffy dads or ordinary high-tone huntin' uncles:

— "They's three ways to booger . . . I mean recycle . . . a tag so's you can use her over and over again till the warden checks you with her hung on a critter or the season's over and you don't need no tag no more. But I ain't tellin' you boys way one. Hard on the game if the competition found out how."

—"Know how the Crees up on the Peace keeps a big old bank beaver from sinkin' in deep, black ice water? Know them fourtenny, twenny ri-twoful over-unders? . . . Naw . . . they find out an' them antis will dry up the supply a them little beauties."

—"Fahr startin'? Rubbin' two boy scouts together's okay, but throwin' in a girl guide's even faster . . . Haw!"

Everyone who has learned from such masters owes it to the great traditions of hunting and fishing to pass the fahr . . . er . . . the torch. For too brief a time it was the honor of Mac and I to instruct Baby Huey, a fine broth of a lad, then in his midtwenties. On the way out to a duck hunt I recall Mac offering to buy one of Huey's huge decoy bags, with which Mac's perverted huntin' dog, Weird, was, even as we haggled, attempting carnal connection.

We loaded Huey with the canoe and both decoy bags and carefully led him the mile and a half into the swamp. Coming out, we loaded him with the canoe, two stringers of ducks and one decoy bag. Baby Huey started to whine.

"Shadd . . . " I started.

"Naw, Bob," Mac interrupted, "Huey's right. It ain't fair he should be unbalanced like that," so Mac handed the kid the second decoy bag. Baby Huey started to sob.

"Gotta pay yer dues, boy," Mac and I said.

In these days of personhood and political correctness we must all remember that females must have equal opportunity to be "brung up right" in the outdoors. Various hunting buddies have told me of their adult daughters expressing resentment that they had never been asked to go, and "that's sexist," etcetera and so on. Most of the dads compound the injustice by saying, "Yup, your Mom was too, in the good old days," or "Whyn't you whine, snivel and pester like your brothers did?"

When I was blessed with a daughter, she was invited and came along just enough to find fly-casting and shooting were so easy they bored her. But what really ended her apprenticeship was the day she proved, in the hearing of her mother, to be a pitch perfect mimic of some of that huntin' and fishin' small talk overheard around a tailgate lunch, to wit: "Slip me some o' that there horse . . . " instead of Miss Manners' preferred "Please pass a portion of the pepperoni."

But my daughter did stay with it long enough to learn some priceless life skills, indoors or out. One day when my hearing was zilch, having forgotten the ear plugs at the range, her uncle Mac taught her the ancient and arcane art of voluntary belching, something that fascinated her more than mere casting and shooting and almost as much as the telephone. She soon taught her best friend (who had such natural talent she instantly became world class) to belch the whole alphabet without reloading.

Back in the days when the girls were seriously figure skating in some arena or another, they were being hit upon big time by some horny hockey players (that is not an oxymoron; there is no other kind). My daughter's friend nearly imploded the dome on her intake "swaller," then cross-checked the louts into the nosebleed seats, chilled their lust and fogged their visors with a belch that blew itself out in the thunderous silence (now, that is an oxymoron) of the rafters.

Sadly we recently learned there may be a downside to the inclusion of women that may finish off what's left of the outdoors apprenticeship system as we know it. It was getting close to the start of the deer season and a hunting buddy had not yet sighted in his rifle. Turned out the appointed day was his to "have" his two small boys. His outdoors-sophisticated spouse explained to me he did not show up because she felt it would be dangerous to have the boys hanging around a range while their dad was concentrating on shooting.

"Hell," I said, "no problem. Mac and I could have taken the boys fishin' maybe, even mushroom huntin', tell them stories, teach them outdoors stuff. . . ."

"That's what I mean," modern mom said, "it was just too dangerous."

4

Alberta, Jugheads and Me

"HARNESS YOUR PEN," THE SIGN NEIGHED TO ALBERTANS fourteen and under, "and in 500 words or less write an essay titled 'The Horse in Alberta.' Use your imagination or past experiences." My eyes filled with tears and an ache came to my heart (not to mention other vital organs) as my imagination began to wrestle my past experience of "Alberta, Jugheads and Me."

It is a miracle how I avoided riding horses so long, growing up in a town where the milk was delivered by a Scot with horse and the freight by métis draymen, also with horses. On a crisp, still day, a small boy with flapping ears could learn to curse in three official languages and two dialects.

Alberta, a lovely seven-year-old tomboy with muscles where other girls didn't even have places, had a pony named Caesar. One day she took me for a ride along with an eight-year-old hulking hunk who had been hanging around vying with me for whatever affection Alberta had left over from horses in general and Caesar in particular. Sweet thing! She assigned hulk the rumble seat for weight distribution, which meant that I, in the middle, got to hug her muscles from the rear.

Instantly we were aboard. Caesar, madly jealous, accelerated fit to whiplash a pronghorn straight toward the windbreak.

"Duck!" yelled Alberta.

I obeyed.

"Where?" queried hulk, craning up to look around. *"Wha
. . . aaaap?"*

Alberta's dad and two big brothers had to use a ladder and
a snatch block to pluck hunk's limp, doubled-up hulk from
where it was draped over that low tree limb like a sweaty horse
blanket on a corral rail. When they had ironed him flat and
whacked some air into him, he showed us he was okay by bel-
lering off home to mama.

Gratefully I slipped Caesar a couple of those everlasting,
gob-stopping jawbreakers. The resulting scar on the pad of my
left palm remains visible to this day to remind me that the
name of this pony should have been Brutus, not Caesar.

After that, what I called my natural horse sense, but what
you might call abject terror, was bolstered by the views of others. William Faulkner wrote somewhere that a mule would toil
for you faithfully for donkey's years just for the chance to kick
you once. Faulkner was himself of the horsy set and could not
bring himself to admit that the poor attitude of the mule
comes from the horse side of the family. One of my favorite
people has an entire quarter section of quarter horses and a
wife one of them busted up taking a dust bath with her still
aboard. My friend gazes at the moiling herd flowing and neigh-
ing over his grazed, bald-headed quarter and says, "Ain't they
purty. . . . You know, keepin' jugheads is okay, just so long as
you never try to ride one of 'em." My friend Griz told me,
"When I get on a horse, he knows instantly who's boss." Me
too, and whenever I regain consciousness the horse and I
always renegotiate the terms of my further employment.

Despite all this wisdom, I booked a sheep hunt several
years ago that required riding horses. So I trained on one of
my sister-in-law's Arabians who jumped its own shadow so

often my body eventually consummated a marriage with its own shadow, flat on the ground. It turned out to be superb training for my hunt with outfitter Dewey Browning. Pepsi, the horse Dewey assigned me, for the twenty-mile trip from the base to the fly camp threw me butt over bald spot into the Clearwater River so many times that I developed diaper rash under my hat. It was probably Pepsi who originated the company slogans ("Pepsi turns you over") or the slow, dirty look and "Don't even think about it."

Dewey said that the part that was hardest on him was not the breaking, training, packing and riding, but the hoss trading he had to do in the off-season to maintain a colorful pinto string like his. He claimed he named Pepsi because that's what he had to drink for three solid days in the marathon session to get him.

Dewey's beloved herself, Neva, dryly noted if that were true, the rest of the string should have names like Old Blue, Rummy, Rye and and Schnapps.

That ride into the fly camp was so rough I vowed I would not dismount even once on the trip back out until I got to the base camp. Stuck to it, too. After only ten miles you could not have separated me from that saddle with turpentine. At base camp they just uncinched and we fell off. I swear I and that saddle wore each other for two weeks.

My other guides and outfitters over the years seemed to favor other modes of transport. Amos Neufeld, for example, drove a chuckwagon. On the trip in to his camp, he put me on a horse that should have been called Piston or even Crankshaft, so world class was she at going up as I was coming down and vicey versey. After only two miles I threw a rod and blew a head gasket. As they loaded me into the chuckwagon, I coined those immortal words: "Let's get back to the wagon boys, these buns is killing me."

Shortly after that I was on the phone to Mike Murphy of Bull Mountain Outfitters, booking the first of my Montana mule deer hunts. It was a done deal, except the touchy part.

"Mike, now about the guarantee. . . ."

"Gol dang it, Bob," Mike exploded, "an outdoors writer like you should know that no reputable outfitter offers guaranteed kills, what's more—"

"Hold on, Mike, I want a no-kill of me guarantee, a guarantee that I do not have to ride a horse."

Mike recalled that he was asked for that one so often he sometimes forgot to mention there was only one cow pony on his whole ranch. The entertainment during my first lunch at the ranch was watching this one throw his beloved owner, Mike's dad, Chuck, clean into a scummy stock tank.

My barber, outfitter Wayne Williams, found me the perfect horse to ride into his base camp. This jughead was twenty-one years old and should have been named *Bonaventure,* because he rode like an aircraft carrier. I tried to buy him.

"Nope," Wayne said. "If ever I get my nerve up again, I got to have something I can ride, don't I?"

What Wayne was riding this trip, having busted a leg on a trail bike, was something I had only been hearing about: it was shiny and bright; it also put-putted, stank and looked like a kiddie car.

"You got the hay burner," Wayne said, "I got the rice burner. This here's your Japanese Jughead, or Tinto Pinto."

I once wrote that a moose was a horse designed by a royal commission. Well, an ATV is merely a moose, copied and redesigned by the Japanese. Actually I jest: the Japanese have striven mightily on the Lord's work of making the horse obsolete as a mode of outdoors travel. But they have done it too well, designing and mass producing the ultimate equine equivalent, even preserving the temperament: the ersatz horse, quad, trike, ATV, whatever you call them, they just will not come.

But every man has his price, and mine was a chance to fish the amazing catch-and-release grayling project on the Little Smoky River with its founder and keeper, Dr. Darryl Smith of Valleyview, Alberta. If he was going to show me, Darryl said, then he was going to show me the best part, which meant eighty miles of alleged road in his 4x4. Then came what Darryl thought was the good news: a sentence of eight to ten miles on his ATV with no chance of early parole.

Dr. Smith had a Kamikaze 500, a 4x4, and an older two-wheel drive Trojan Horse model I named "Old Two." Soon we came to a deep gully and berm designed to stop vehicle traffic on a pipeline right-of-way. I suggested I should study Darryl's technique taking my Old Two through. Suddenly there was the great grandmother of overdone wheelies, and I cursed for not having my camera ready. Had I done so, I would have had a priceless shot of machine and Darryl, his hat still on, hanging upside down from the lower point of a sickle moon in the late morning sky, a shot every manufacturer would have paid me big bucks not to publish. Then the sky hook straightened and everything crashed upside down in the gully with a clap like thunder. Dust settled; somewhere a wood tick tittered nervously. I fretted into the silence about the nerve of some people getting themselves killed, leaving me without the slightest idea how to find my way out of this mess.

But we outdoors writers are intrepid and resourceful. "Is there a doctor in the horse?" I asked the wreck of Trojan Horse and equipment. (If I didn't, I should have; never waste a good line.)

Darryl crawled out, gave me one of those Pepsi looks and did not really lighten up until we had set up camp and were catching grayling on every cast. His mood elevated even more two days later when Old Two reared up on the way out and buried me under machine and load until we resembled an aboriginal funeral mound.

When I surfaced, the doctor observed (or would have, had he been an outdoors writer) that he should have brought the tombstone he saw once, which was inscribed: "Here lies an outdoors writer and a human being."

"But, nah," Darryl said, "there isn't room for two people under that wreck."

The last words on the subject of my friend Griz came to

me: "As between a riderless horse and an ATV plus rider, the horse has more total brains . . . barely."

Whoa! Those old hosses Experience and Imagination have run away with us. But, by the time I was fourteen, I could not have kept myself to 500 words on the contest topic unless I forgot them and concentrated on history, sociology and other trivialities, as follows. . . .

Nobody could have predicted how important to the future of Alberta was the decision of the Royal Northwest Mounted Police to establish a major horse ranch at Pincher Creek in 1881. First, the Blackfeet took the horses from the police, founding a whole industry. As the *Canadian Encyclopedia* says: "Horses moved from one tribe to another, generally by theft." Thus, the Bloods and the Cree stole the jugheads from the Blackfeet, and so on. Horses became a form of currency by which natives displayed their wealth. Inherently the horses were as worthless as their descendants, today's "wild" horses, or even our Loonie, which is made round to go round, and just as fast.

But the braves did play this game for keeps, and the maiming and killing of winners and losers alike in these "horse trades" insured that only the horses, not the native peoples, survived to overpopulate their range. Ironically, the natives did not notice until it was too late the plague of exotic humanity (settlers) that was even then arriving, overpopulating and over-running the natives' range. Today the descendants of many of those settlers keep poodles and otherwise divert themselves and their wealth from doing any real conservation work by "adopting" alleged "wild" horses to prevent them being converted to . . . poodle food. Inevitably most of them will just have to break and then try to ride their "wild" and "free" creatures. That will ensure that their kind, too, will become extinct, and that their beasts run free again. What goes around, comes around . . . and around . . . and around.

5

Vested Interests

A FISHING VEST IS A SLEEVELESS GARMENT WITH MAZES OF pockets and pouches in which fly-fishermen can hopelessly misplace the multitudes of items they do not need anyway. It was one of the early inventions of the young Lee Wulff, who died in 1991. Several years before he died I had the opportunity to thank the great one himself, not only because of the way the vest permits the fly-fisherman to keep both hands free, but also because we sociologists of angling can tell more than we really need to know about a person from the kind of vest he has, its condition and what he loses in those pockets.

It is an industry secret that all fishing vests are made by a single antifishing misanthrope in Hong Kong. The vests are then shipped to the U.S.A., where the label is put on and the price tripled before they are shipped hither and yon, even to Japan. It is only a matter of time until the label inside the collar will be replaced by the big manufacturer's logo on the back of every vest. Yuppie perfection will be attained when every wearer is obliged to advertise precisely who imported this ridiculous garment.

Just for starters, almost every fishing vest you see is made of such shiny, almost white cloth that it is one of the better fish repellents, ranking with those clunking stream cleats and the white Tilley hat. Should you accidentally stumble upon a human wearing a camouflage vest and hat, blending into the underbrush and impersonating an old stump, beware! Check your location! You have either bumped into the late Charlie Brooks, West Yellowstone angling author of consummate skill and cunning, or you have stumbled upon the rare, canny old veteran still among us here on *terra firma* who has the money to get his vests custom-made or the time to get them artfully aged, faded and soiled in camouflagelike patches.

All fishing vests that have been worn even once will be heavily soiled in the vicinity of one particular pocket: the one used to store the fly dope (not the insect repellent), the dry fly floatant. Fly floatant illustrates the prime principle of marketing to fly-fishermen: take a common substance the world produces in abundance, divide it into minuscule quantities, give it a dumb name (*Fink*, for example), multiply its price a thousandfold and sell it like hot . . . no . . . like dope to addicts. Better yet, sell it in a container cunningly designed to leak under all conditions and positions and you will sell even more of it. All the technology of the industry is now concentrated on the tendency of some floatants to solidify below 95° F. If they could make it remain liquid and leaking day and night, profits would double or triple.

Should you encounter astream any human wearing a fishing vest without the filthy stain on that one pocket, he is either a land surveyor, a timber cruiser or the only nonpurist in the world who does not either fish only the dry fly or claim to. In this latter case, the whole vest may be full of fly sinkant, another dumb name for a noxious substance: (called *Dunk* or *Dink*) divided, subdivided, price multiplied, etcetera, as with floatant, but for some reason the manufacturers have not yet perfected a container that will faithfully and reliably leak sinkant.

Small quantities of substances more expensive per ounce even than single malt whiskey, both to make floating flies sink and sinking flies float, also will *be lost* somewhere in virtually every vest worn by any fly-fisherman. But that fact in no way exhausts the propensity of fly-fishermen to guzzle snake oil. A caution: to blame the manufacturers and dealers would be as unjust as to blame the snake for the product rendered from its mortal remains. *Caveat emptor* of yourself!

Exhibit A, somewhere, in a growing number of fishing vests, will be a tiny container of a new wonder substance to take the shine off a new leader; it also makes floating flies sink. Its dumb name? *Mud.* Something found in natural abundance and free along every trout stream I have frequented anywhere in the world. My case against the dope trade to fly dopes and other substance abusers not only rests, it is prostrate.

The sociologist neither experienced with anglers nor, God forbid, an angler himself could be forgiven for expecting that somewhere in any fly-fisherman's vest there will be two flies: one floating fly so the owner can buy sinkant, yea, even Mud, and one sinking fly so the owner can properly develop the stain on that one pocket of the vest, the badge of the Fink addict. You can rest assured that any native fly-fisher will have two flies. There will be one on the leader, as local wisdom insists that the best lure for Rocky Mountain whitefish is a wet fly "sweetened" by a maggot. There will be a second fly some-where in that vest, tackle box or creel in case the first is lost. If the second is lost? No problem, the nearest Bait and Jig Boutique is only five dollars worth of gas away, and they sell Japanese wet flies for twenty-nine cents. But if what we have is a real, unsweetened fly-fisherman, there will be hundreds, thou-sands, maybe even millions of flies in boxes and bottles every-where in that vest.

All those flies are tickets to gamble against the "theory of selectivity," invented by outdoors writers, a game with more combinations and permutations than Lotto 6/49. These writers credit the trout with the palate of a professional wine taster, the eyesight of a bonefish guide and the intelligence of an Einstein. For a long while I believed that the writers produced this stuff because the quarry would not be worthy of the fishing or the writing about it if not imbued with superhuman qualities. But gradually, as I get to know more and more angling writers, I have come, sadly, to suspect that the theory of selectivity may have something to do with the simple fact that so many of them are also in the business of peddling fly dope and flies, or, worse, books on aquatic entomology.

In my slush pile, I have a superb article called "The Petit Jury," in which I argue that a "jury" of only six fly patterns will cover any angler for better than 90 percent of all the conditions he will encounter on any water in North America. I proudly once told a writer and tackle dealer friend about this article. When he recovered consciousness, he excused himself to make a few phone calls. This article, somehow, has never been published, but has earned me ten times in kill fees what it would bring if ever printed, even in one of the big three of the hook and bullet press. The article is like a banking card: any time I'm broke I stick it in the slot, sometimes to a publisher who has already paid me kill fees for it. No matter, back it comes with a kill fee. I wonder who my writer and dealer friend had to phone so urgently that he had to do it even after being so suddenly sick like that? My final word on the millions of flies in the vest of a real fly-fishermen is this: fly-fishing itself is founded on the capacity for self-delusion of a beautiful, wild creature with a brain the size of a pea; the fly-fishing industry is based likewise on the similar capacity of the beautiful dopes addicted to fly-fishing.

The vest of any real fly-fisherman will likely contain more

glassine envelopes than a dope peddler's stash, but these will contain leaders; there will also be dozens of tiny spools of material to construct still more leaders. Leaders and their design are subjects fraught with more depressing formulae and schools of thought than nuclear physics. There is the very rare school that believes most trout just do not care, that therefore the best leader tippet to use is one of the largest diameter that will squeeze through the eye of the hook. But there is a warning: if you spot a person astream who appears to be pulling cobwebs from the sky, rolling them up and measuring thin air with a $600 micrometer and muttering darkly in mathematics, take my advice and leave. This person is of the schizophrenic school of leader design, which believes if it is strong enough to hold any fish, then it is too thick to fool him in the first place. These maniacs strive always for the longest, strongest, thinnest leader, and are revolted by the very feel of trout in the hand; thus, they never have use for net or creel as they specialize in the thirty-foot release.

There will probably be no room in that vest to lose anything else, after dope, leaders, tippets and flies are stowed. Researchers will then have to study what is hung on the vest and about the person of the subject. If there is a thermometer prominently displayed, for example, what you have is a person who does not even know the best time to go fishing is when the boss or his wife says he can go. Most people who own water thermometers either do not know how to use them or cannot remember the best temperature ranges for the various species of trout. You should always let your fly, leader and line trail downstream as you kneel for the minute or so necessary to get a reading. If you get a fish on that dragging fly, something that happens so often I call it a thermometer fish, it is definitely the right time to go fishing. If you do not get a thermometer fish, you can carry on fishing against all odds, or you can use your thermometer to see if the beer is cold enough to drink yet.

There may be a set of forceps clipped onto some protuberance of the vest. This device is an ambiguous sign. It can mean that the wearer fully intends to release the fish should he ever manage to catch it. On the other hand, he could be a lost urologist, and you should back up against the nearest cliff and clap your hands over your privates. If the forceps are distinguished by that dull sheen, that patina of heavy use, it means only that this is one of those boneheads who habitually fishes in the company of his bird dog and that dog is back in the bush looking for yet another porcupine to eat so his master can ply those forceps once again to pulling quills.

Other ambiguous signs are the presence or absence of nets and creels, both of which have become controversial since catch and release became politically correct. Clearly the old-fashioned wicker creel is passé, the only purpose of such an antique being as obvious as that of the crematoria at Dachau. Some people can get away with a small canvas creel. If challenged, the owner will swear he only uses it to carry out the litter abandoned by other anglers. Even much-beloved Charlie Brooks was held in suspicion in some quarters because he favored a huge canvas water bag with the top cut off and a shoulder strap added. One day I went on a safari with Charlie to the third Barn Hole on the Madison and recalled, after I regained consciousness, that he could transport and cool en route in the desert no less than a flat "24" of what it was he carried in that creel. Dimly I recall Charlie saying, "If you can carry them out empty, you can carry them in full." But then, Charlie never could be serious about equipment or a cliché.

Nets are optional. Strangely the most crazed fish-releasers who completely reject creels find nets acceptable, especially if they are very tiny, hand sculpted and cost more than a Van

Gogh original. If the reason given for wearing one of these things is that it makes it easier to release fish, you know you are talking to a very modern fly-fisherman. Those cheap aluminum nets hung from a rubber cord around the neck are out, for a very practical reason: if you look closely at habitual users, they will have no front teeth, the result of having turned around to see where the net was tangled in the bush just as it wasn't anymore. That is the reason such persons now carry the lethal thing stuffed down the waders.

Actually, while in England for the World Fly-Fishing Championship, I learned to favor those marvelous Norwegian folding nets that the British have to conjure like a silk hanky from the sleeve of their tweed jackets because the Brits do not favor fishing vests at all. With the extension handle of these folders, they can net any fish out there at the farthest end of their cast that is even thinking about taking their fly.

Certainly you will hear no British angler going on about the use of these nets in releasing fish, a practice they regard as bad form and even a tad vulgar, like breaking wind anywhere, let alone in your own waders, which is why the Brits don't wear them much, either. But then you do not need to judge British anglers by what they wear or use: they all have to be upper-class, or at least stinking rich to be fishing in the first place. . . .

6

Zero Impact Logging

Iт was as fine a Labor Day as ever was. The ribs were fragrant in the water-smoker, the women were off on a nature hike and my friend Griz and I were idling on my Stump Ranch porch, trying to rev up our nerve.

"Now, I'm not saying we will," Griz said, "but we'd have to take out that front one first . . . give those back two a clear fall."

Generally you agree with Griz, so I nodded wisely. We had been psyching ourselves up ever since the windy night the previous hunting season when we woke, seasick, in a thumping, squeaking and rocking cabin.

When the cabin was built I told the contractor not to fell any more trees than absolutely essential. He, being a good Canadian, did not know the difference between scratching his behind and tearing it all to jerky, and actually left a three-foot notch in one of the eaves for two adolescent aspens he thought looked cute. But the trees, just as cute kittens will, grew up: now they rubbed the wall like horny bull moose and, swaying in a wind, levered the cabin up and down on its cement piles.

Why "Stump Ranch?" people wonder. Besides peace, quiet, brown trout, ruffed grouse and deer, organic stumps are the only product of the place. Here zero impact logging means no stumps on purpose, that the only sawlogs snaked into the pile are stolen from beavers and the sawn chunks are then split into firewood, preferably by someone else.

Whenever we have as guests a couple of those good old Canadian boys who have removed themselves from the bush, but from whom the bush can never be cleared, I remark sadly how splitting is a lost art any more, then stand back. They say any man who splits his own firewood is warmed twice, but a man, horizontal in his hammock with a book and a beer, listening to a splitting contest at his woodpile, is a thousand times warm all over.

Modern bush boys are off planting pot or something instead of trapping for their college money as they did back in my and Griz's day. Along my trapless crik the great Canadian rodent constantly cruises for timber, closer and closer to my cabin and power line. Preventing a beaver from dropping a tree on either is one of the few reasons we ever purposely create a stump.

Those two aspens in the eaves, two tons each of standing sap, were a frightening challenge. Drop one backwards and the cabin is kindling; too far right and it's the biffy in flinders; a hair left of dead center snaps the power line. We feared accomplishing on purpose what were trying to prevent some dumb rodent from doing instinctively.

Griz stepped to the edge of the deck and stared off into space for a while, then he studied his cigarette smoke drifting straight up. "Hell, it's a good day to die, let's do her," he announced.

Griz and I differ on the theory and practice of precision tree felling. I always lash a snatch block to the base of a tree down in the falling zone, double the winch line through it and around the victim as high as possible, then hide Newt, my old Landcruiser, in the background somewhere, winch a good bend in the tree, notch, saw, then run like hell. As Andy Russell says

about yelling at charging Grizzly bears: it has always worked—
so far. But Griz always sneers, "Real loggers don't winch."

So I knew it was serious when Griz's own idea was we
would have to use the winch on these trees. But not my way.
No way, said Griz, not enough line speed with the cable doubled through the snatch block, or something. Vehicle and
winch had to be straight down the combat zone and he'd wave
when to hit her. Hell, who was I, a prairie lad, seven before I
saw my first sapling, to argue with someone who was raised on
a stump ranch?

The big saw snarls, Griz waves, I winch, then too many
things seem to happen suddenly, but in slow motion. The tree
hangs in the fluffy clouds, then topples straight at me and
Newt. Fortunately a gust of wind twists the top foliage like a
kite on a tight string, left, toward the power line. At center
stage, Griz's cap spins lazily in the air, like a stalled Frisbee.
Then comes a *twang* like a bowstring and Griz enters the film's
frame from stage right, soaring, like an arrow over the parking
lot, one hand shading his eyes, scouting the softest landing.

When the dust settled it was clear my friend had neither
been catapulted by the base of the tree nor shot from a bow.
He had merely been running a dive play getaway. The twang
had been either Griz tripping over the ladder or the power pole
bending, then the line snapping. At first I could not find Griz,
then I heard a groan. He had hit, then joined my woodpile.
Old Griz was the saw log oozing the red sap.

"Lucky she didn't fall straight," I said. "We mistriangulat-
ed and she'd have totaled old Newt." I have heard and seen
many strange things around woodpiles, but never before has
one uttered such profanity.

After we figured out how the ladies could cook dinner
without electricity, I spent the rest of the afternoon trying to
restore Griz's nerve. After all, I argued, the power line was

already down; all we had to worry about now was felling those eaves trees away from the cabin because, anyhow, we were out of kindling and could use a new biffy.

"No," Griz said, "it is not a good day to d. . . to do that." My distinct impression was no day was a good day for us to fell the eaves aspens, so I called Spike, a lineman for the power company, who lived nearby and moonlighted in troublesome trees. Spike warned me his moon had eclipsed recently in a treetop, but he'd come out Sunday and consult.

About noon a gaunt gent hobbled down my driveway, supported by a pretty wife. "Busted up felling one from the top down," Spike explained. "Topping trees is God telling you you're all balls and no brains." He inspected the eaves trees.

"You do this?" he asked.

"No, the carpenter."

"Bubble from his level must of went to his brain," Spike said. "No sweat, we'll dump 'em as soon as I hook your line back up."

"Er . . . maybe we should fell 'em, then hook the line back up," I suggested.

"Any idiot, even you, could miss just the biffy. We pros need challenge." When the wiring was finished he asked, "Got a winch for that rig? Snatch block?"

So we dropped the eaves aspens exactly the way prairie boys usually do it, with Newt hid behind the cabin and the winch line doubled. Faster than you could holler t-i-m-b-e-r, those great living standpipes of waterlogged pulpwood were laid out stiff, straight and peaceful as dead preachers, dead center on a line between the biffy and the power line. Zero impact, except on the ground, no twang and hold the kindling. My money was no good, but Spike hinted he and "the old lady" had always admired my south piece and wondered about deer hunting permission down there.

"You got it," I said.

"You what? Griz yelled when I told him all this two or three weeks later, as we were doing some preseason deer scouting down there.

"What next?" Griz went on, "Let one local in here, then you know they'll all be hunting that big old buck of ours, and just when I was about to tell you this is a good day to figger out how to move the cabin and leave those eaves aspens be."

7

It's Fishing—Cats and Dogs

FAT CATS DON'T HUNT, GOES THE SAYING. BUT DO THEY FISH? I caught my first chub in years the other day, which reminded me that the best fishing dog I ever knew was a cat, a skinny black cat named Fever, short for Hay Fever because she sneezed so much and because that is what I hollered at her later in our partnership when I wanted her to know it was time to go fishing.

Fever was a product of evolution of the fifty or so generations of cats that had occupied my father-in-law's barn ever since the day he built it. Like all barn cats, they preyed and were preyed upon. There will never be a shortage of coyotes and cougars as long as people will insist on raising a surplus of things like poodles and domestic cats. But even the coyotes were not enough; occasionally my father-in-law had to disappear for a while with his Cooey .22 and a gunny sack. That chore and porcupine control were the only hunting he ever did.

A fishing cat is so rare it is too bad I cannot remember precisely how it all got started. As best as I recall, I found Fever in my creel a time or two, snuffling and sneezing around in there like it had been full of catnip. Eventually, I know, I got around to leaving in the creel one or two of the chubs that would take my worms in the crik in those days.

What happened next at least proved this was a cat that could add smell and creel and get chub. Wife, mother and sister-in-law all thought it was so cute that I am sure there are pictures in three households of this scenario from way back when: me, booted and hatted for fishing, with Fever either at heel or skipping happily ahead, no farther than my longest cast away, following or leading that fragrant creel up the creek.

Fever was black, but though she crossed my path many times, she was never bad luck. She was wild and hungry as a wolverine, like all barn cats, but she would sit there and watch intently, black tail swishing, and only occasionally *myowlaaachoo* in outrage as I caught and released, or creeled the odd trout, until eventually I would catch and throw her a chub.

All this was long before I owned my first hunting dog, a Brittany named Quince, who came along about the same time as our first child. In those days I regarded the concept of the fishing dog as a harmless form of insanity that possessed most new dog owners. But, since from about the time he was three I had to take son John fishing, I thought I might as well try to turn Quince into a fishing dog at the same time, which is like saying that since you already have a hurricane you might at well get a typhoon, too. Quince was the greatest hunting dog I have ever seen. Just show him what you wanted him to hunt and he'd do it, but he was just your average fishing dog, which means he was plain awful.

Hunting dogs usually perform their specialty when you take them fishing, the distinction between a fishing rod and a shotgun being something that no dog seems able to grasp. Retrievers will swim around flushing most of the fish, but when they miss one and you accidentally manage to catch it, they will try to help you land it, which is worse, far worse than that infernal helpful soul who invariably materializes from nowhere with his net, just in time to "help" by knocking a world record whatever off your hook.

Bird dogs, hounds and that ilk spend some time paddling around doing Labrador imitations, hunting and flushing fish, but when you roar at them, they sulk off hunting for real. I mind the time young Kurt Browning went out to feed father Dewey's cougar pack and forgot to latch the gate. It was then and there, in that kennel gateway west of Caroline, not in any foreign arena or in world competition, that the young skating superstar executed the world's first high, spinning, quadruple jump. There was a brief holocaust of his mother's bantam chicken flock, then the phone calls started from Nordegg to the west, Sundre to the south, Drayton Valley to the north, Eckville to the east, which is to say, from the entire civilized world: "Dewey . . . Heard 'em in the night. They was headin' northwest. Sounded fine. . . . Real purty."

The last hound straggled in ten days later, just as Kurt and the final feather from the bantam explosion were wafting to earth. This is true; I do not exaggerate, but I do digress to make the important point that, given any opening or excuse at all, hunting dogs just have to go hunting.

Old Quince and the other dogs since with which I have not learned my lesson about fishing were not quite that bad. Late in the day they'd come back bearded with porcupine quills, and I'd have to cut short a fishing trip to get into East Anguish just in time to ruin the nearest vet's, Doc Spavins', Saturday night. Quince once returned carrying the only rooster from a neighbor lady's chicken flock. To this day she must wonder why they got a turkey for Christmas since there is no fishing water on their land. The dog had a good eye: that rooster had a fine ginger neck cape for fly tying, but that's another whole story. . . .

Generally old Quince would stick around, worrying. He always thought I was irresponsible and believed someone would have to look after John when I was deep in research for yet another fishing column. They would dismantle log jams and beaver dams to get the logs to throw for Quince to retrieve.

One day my swinging wet fly tangled in the thick hair behind the pup's collar when he was trying to retrieve a log or flush a fish. I decided to teach him a lesson by playing and landing him, but he climbed up on a midstream rock and lay doggo there and I had to break him off. My old fishing buddy Vern Caddy tried to teach the same lesson to a beaver he hooked one night on an especially nasty section of the South Raven. To paraphrase the old saying, he returneth late at night, smelling not of strong drink, but of blood and the black mud known as Loon S . . . t, needing a strong drink, and more truth was in him than we needed to hear.

But there we go digressing again. . . . Landing and releasing strange catches is the subject for another whole column. Occasionally when John and Quince had cleared the entire watershed of logjams and beaver dams to the point of causing flash floods downstream in Fort Kindling, only then would they watch the fishing. In fact Quince would staunchly point the fragrant road kills I call dry flies as they floated along.

While he was doing this one day, a very large brown trout swallowed the thing. Steady to wing and shot though he was on upland birds, Quince broke point on this fish, barking, yipping and zipping back and forth like a shuttle in and out of the warp and woof of the stripped-in fly line below my rod hand. Somehow I let John net the fish, then upped and flung Quince in the river, the better to untangle the fabric into which he had woven the line.

Immediately John emitted a long wail that had me scanning the skies for the bombers of a nuclear attack. The kid was twenty-one before he confessed to me that he had not known until that moment what I meant when I so often quoted one of the maxims his granddad lived by: "Take a boy fishing, and throw the little b . . . d in."

In theory at least I have learned my lesson about fishing dogs, but hundreds of anglers never do. Umpty ump times a season you will encounter a brother angler accompanied by a dog. Make sure you get far enough out of the way to avoid becoming an ingredient in a backlash, but not so far as to impair your enjoyment of the creative cursing that is sure to fill the fresh air soon.

Why I did not even know my father-in-law ever uttered an oath until one evening I was fishing behind that barn long after Fever had made some coyote's day and passed on to that great chub fishery in the sky. The old boy was trying to get Sweetheart, his last milk cow, into the barn to be milked. Trouble was, Sweetheart was one of those cows all anglers are familiar with who like to follow you up the crik, doing their raging bull imitation and keeping you in the water until your waders pucker, inside and out. Behind the barn was a diamond willow thicket so dense you couldn't find yourself in there with a mirror and a spotlight. Great thrashings and cursings came from in there as the old man tried to find and flush Sweetheart. The syntax was out of sync, but it sure was sincere: "(Organic fertilizer) . . . (unnatural act)-all . . . double (Deity) damn you Sweetheart . . . you son of a (mother of all dogs, particularly fishing dogs)."

But a loud *myowlaaachoo* brought me back to the chore at hand. I swear in the gloom of the dusk up on the bank there, old Fever was grinning from ear to ear.

8

Serious What-tail Bizness

WHEN I ARRIVED FOR ONE OF MY MONTANA DEER HUNTS, the president of Warren and Sweat, Dr. Ray McIntyre, of Grand Island, Florida, was already in camp and busy with another boss's dirty job: testing his own tree stands against a couple of "book" whitetails he had spotted in the Musselshell River bottom.

For a change one morning, his guide drove Ray around the mule deer areas of the ranch. They spotted the sure "book" mule buck that I had named Horseshoes the first of the three seasons I had been hunting him. As the frustrated guide put it, "But Doc won't goin' blow his tag on no mule."

Dr. Ray himself told me, simply, "Bob, what-tails is serious bizness." How serious? You have to know Ray gave up a dental practice to pursue big bucks in tree stands. It would be bad for business for Ray's new business to take even a Boone & Crockett mulie while riding around in a clapped-out, camo Suburban called Desert Storm.

Many supremely successful whitetail trophy hunters are abject failures at serious what-tail bizness. My friend Barry Mitchell, publisher of the *Alberta Fishing Guide*, religiously follows the gospel writ by the gurus of the modern whitetail cult. In August each year he tunes his bow as though it were a

Stradivarius. He practices safe scouting wearing camo chest waders and leaving no scent when he is "locating the dominant buck," then "programming" him and finding his "core area" and other buzzwords of the meticulous—compulsive whitetail hunter.

Only then does he hang enough treestands to produce Boone & Crockett balance sheets for people like Ray McIntyre. I was with Barry one evening a few years ago while he spurred his way up an aspen to hang his seventeenth stand so high that I toppled over backwards into my own nosebleed just watching him climb.

All bow season Mitchell nested from can to can't see in one stand or another, using one bottle for potty and occasionally sipping water from what he hoped was the other.

To Mitchell's nose, the attractant scents industry exudes a powerful odor of mendacity. But he does hang his full camo clothes outside camp in a gunny sack sweetened with wild sage, pine needles, even pure, fresh, green alfalfa pellets concentrated by the deer themselves from organic materials; mustn't have the uniform contaminated with the familiar fumes inside any good deer camp: whiskey, beans, smoke, beans, wet wool, whiskey, more beans. . . . He became so scent-challenged from bathing in baking soda that bloodhounds could not track him between that gunny sack and the deer camp biffy.

The lad also keeps meticulous records. In eleven previous bow seasons, all in Alberta's prime northern whitetail country, he has had more than 200 bucks come within his absolute maximum range, twenty-seven in the '87 season alone. But in all that time he had chanced only two shots, missing both.

Yet, in that time, Mitchell has collected a wall of trophy heads to die for, which is just what those whitetails did, but all by the rifle, after he had hung up his bow for the last time for yet another year.

But in 1993 Barry could not get done with his best trout season ever. What he bent all summer were fly rods, not bows. Nary a buck did he program nor an area core. On opening day of archery season Mitchell was still chasing cold-blooded quarry down on his beloved Crowsnest River. A week later he finally decided to venture out to one or another of his last year's stands.

Halfway in he remembered everything he forgot. So he laid down everything he had remembered and trudged the quarter mile back to his rig and drove to camp for his finger tabs, arm guard and hat. Then he drove back and huffed and puffed the additional quarter mile to the tree in which his stand was still hanging.

Mitchell tied the whizzle string, umbilical cord (or whatever it is archers call it), to his load, then climbed up. But he had not attached the other end to himself. Down. Up. Then he found he had left his ditty bag, twong pouch (or whatever), down there. Down again and up, one more time.

By this time his thermostat was stuck. He steamed like a muskeg fire. The aspen seemed in spring bloom again, so fuzzy were its bare branches with Barry's humid effluvium.

Then Barry discovered his bow hanger was hanging . . . down there, too. He snapped off a limb on a neighboring aspen and hung the bow on the stub. He was at least an hour and a half late now, anyway, and had anyhow sent sound and scent alarms from there to the correction line. A good evening, he thought, to get nothing but fresh air and sunset. He got out his trash novel of Mafia doings and did something he never does while on stand—lit a cigarette to spice his scent cloud. But things did quiet down quickly. Somewhere, in fact, a mushroom cracked the Earth's crust; the new-born fungus heard only flipping pages and heavy breathing.

Barry Mitchell was into his second cigarette and through

half a chapter when his concentration on a fictional steamy scene was interrupted by a sound he now describes as halfway between a doe blow and a buck snort. He looked up to see a real steamy scene—a very good buck making mud pies; Barry had not even known a scrape was there.

Then Mitchell commenced arm-wrestling his quiver for an arrow until he remembered the only one that would come loose. He knackered it (or whatever archers call it), drew and released in one jerk and errored the beast straight and true through the liver and lights. The only thing he did right was remember you do not walk on air out of the tree stand even after you have taken your first buck with the bow. Within fifty yards he found his trophy. The antlers green-scored 158 6/8s Boone and Crockett points. Don't we all wish I was making this up?

Mitchell's season was over, so he had to buy the whiskey and bake the beans, plus wash the dishes for the rifle hunters in his camp. I tried to comfort him with quotations from the gospel writ by some of the idols of the what-tail bizness, such as: "As between good and lucky, I'll take lucky ever' time."

"But," Barry asks, "isn't convincing them you aren't even hunting them part of 'good', too? . . . It is . . . isn't it?"

Maybe, but the story is bad for the whitetail mystique and illustrates that Barry Mitchell, though a superb a whitetail hunter, knows no more than the rest of us about "Serious What-tail Bizness." By now anyone who was not one error shy of a full quiver would be cashing in: writing a book, working title, *Accidental Whitetails—On Purpose*, or at least doing endorsements for that cigarette brand.

9

Down On the Farm Boys

IN A RECENT HARD WINTER A GROUP OF LAWYERS MET TO BREAK bread and trade tricks. One asked if we had noticed how the friendly neighborhood rapist, child molester, sniper, etcetera, always turned out to be one of "those nice quiet kids next door," and how were we going to, pray God, be delivered from them?

Then a front-runner on life's fast track mentioned he had recently been up shoveling the roof of his $250,000 split level. Several of the gents and ladies were horrified.

"No problem," fast track said, "I'm an old farm boy."

Sometimes the term used is "old country boy." No matter which, the only people I know who do not wish to be delivered of either are the select group of orthopedic surgeons and morticians who do very well on the fast track specializing in dealing with the remains of people who shovel their own roofs.

There is one way of distinguishing a genuine good old farm boy from a country boy: the farm boy will wear his free tractor store ball hat straight ahead, and his laces will be done up.

In fact, the farm boy may be one of the only kids you will see these days who does not wear runners. He will wear what they did in my day, what my mother called clod hoppers and other complimentary names that just made us envious at the way these lads kicked and slid along, striking sparks from concrete, gravel, and occasionally from each other's heads and other more vital organs.

Jeans will have the snoose ring on the arse pocket, which, I suspect, may be stone-bleached in at the factory. One farm boy I know claimed his daddy taught him never to go to the bank without cow doo on his boots. With that snoose can and a small brush, he always has a handy supply. "Chew it or do it," he says. "Don't make no never mind, except snoose smells worse."

But farm boy—country boy is no matter: they are all convinced in their own minds that they can do anything with their hands. In fact, they almost have the rest of us convinced that they are, well, "handy," from the number of fingers they don't have on those hands.

Mortician's question: "How many farm boys does it take to grease a combine?"

Answer: "Just one, if you run him through slow."

Certainly farm boys spend a lot of time in the outdoors; the assumption is they are so expert in the skills involved that every outdoors expedition should include a farm boy or two.

To hear them tell it, every former farm boy put himself through graduate school by running a trapline when he was a kid. Maybe, but the only person I know who parked his rig by a half-done beaver tree and came back to find the truck totaled by the well-done tree was a farm boy. Now most of the farm boys I know have turned to drier, more rewarding work, to pure agriculture, cultivating pot on the back forty.

Farm boys share with land surveyors a touching faith in their sense of direction. As the group split up for a long, still-hunting drive at Camp Wainwright one snowy day, I asked if everyone had a compass.

"Naw," said one, "I'm an old country boy."

After what we learned that afternoon, I now always answer that one with: "Which country?"

With one tracking and two trying to head him off, my recollection is we caught our farm boy—wild-eyed and lathered—just after sundown on the outskirts of Saskatoon. He had jogged across dozens of roads and trails, and even two paved highways without pausing, to get there.

Now these guys get a choice: take the compass or be chained to the fire hydrant I always have in the rig.

Animals. Farm boys always know everything there is to know about them, particularly your dog. Giving a pitying look to your purebred, registered, trained Brittany, every mother's son of them will tell you about the coyote-poodle cross he had as a lad that was the best damn hunting dog there ever was, never had a lesson in his life. . . . I always interrupt to ask how *long* that life was. What with coyote hunters, poisoners, other farmers protecting their flocks, city drivers on country roads and reckless rockers on the verandah, no free-range farm dog survives its second year.

Shoot? Everyone knows all farm boys are natural master marksmen. Yet the worst shot I have ever known is a good old country boy who brags that he has not missed in fifteen years. Right on! It's that long since he missed a whole magazine at his last bear, which, he swears to this day, was charging him, when the fact is he was merely standing in the way of where the bear wanted to go in a hurry. Now, for fifteen years, this one has been an avocational naturalist, wandering around in the woods with an empty rifle or, somehow, never managing to get his safety off in time.

As an adult I kept the rifle of my youth, a single shot Cooey with a gorgeous "browned" finish from the manure pile under which I hid it from my Dad, who believed nonfarm boys should not have their own rifles. It featured a rear sight I gun-smithed from the tin band of a shingle bundle. It could never be touched because it would bend and because I knew if I aimed exactly four inches high and two to the right at fifty yards I could execute every gopher from here to the correction line.

One day my friend Griz saw it in my rack and fell in love. It reminded him of the one that was always filthy, always loaded in the rack of his Dad's pickup; the one Griz had used to shoot enough beavers to put himself through graduate school, then become a college teacher, so he too could shovel his own roof and make orthopods and morticians rich. He had to try it.

He missed the first shot at a gopher. "Hmmm," he grunt-ed, and instantly held precisely four inches high, two to the right, and the second shot transmogrified that rodent into a lit-tle pink cloud blowing east.

Griz just had to have the rifle. Some former farm boys call themselves good old country boys. They dress better than farm boys and are shrewd enough to take advantage of the rest of us by constantly reminding us of their backwoods backgrounds. Griz talked me out of the rifle by the simple expedient of tear-ful stories of his heritage, then continually offering me more and more money until I got embarrassed at taking advantage of a friend.

By breakup one year he decided he wanted a gorgeous new repeating bolt action "twenny ri-twoful." But with typical shrewdness in matters economic he vowed he would have to pay for that new rifle with beaver pelts taken with the old Cooey. By then beaver trapping, skinning, fleshing, stretching, etcetera, had dropped to about ten cents an hour and most pros had turned to regular jobs, like chicken plucking in the local fryer factory.

One late spring evening I walked over to see Griz, maybe have a pop or two and watch the Stanley Cup final game on his big screen while he did his usual—letting only the instant replays interrupt his fly tying. The garage doors were wide open, the lights inside ablaze. At the end of the driveway, out on the street several nice-looking ladies were pacing, holding scented hankies over their cute little noses and "generous" mouths.

"Oooh, I don' go fa dis," one snuffled. "Didn' fum duh staht." Seems that morning Griz had flung his garage doors open, and the fumes caused almost everyone to evacuate the neighborhood. The exceptions were the husbands, spousal equivalents or facsimiles or whatever we call them these days; no matter, the ripe, musky fumes attracted them like flies to swarm around that open garage door.

I looked in the door and there were half a dozen gents grimly whittling away at a pile of Beaver carcasses, skinning, sharpening, fleshing, sharpening, stretching. Griz was not among them.

That worthy was down in his rec room, just tying off an exquisite #22 Bastard Adams and trading insults with Don Cherry.

"What's that all about?" I nodded in the general direction of Griz's garage.

"A male encounter group discovering their roots?" he replied.

"Come on, how come you're in here doing your spring usual and they're out there hacking away at your pile of beaver?"

"I swear," Griz said, the sure sign he was lying, "that I was just going to get started on all them beaver corpses, when a whole bunch of my neighbor gents turned up at my garage door, so I invited them in to watch."

"You didn't say anything else?"

"Well I might have allowed as how there ain't many people left in this modern civilization who still have the old skills." Griz has his M.A. in English, which means he knows how to let his language slip a notch when he is doing his country boy bit.

"Suppose you did say something like that, what was the response?"

"Amazing, just amazing. Seems to have touched a nerve. There was this whole hymn of 'I grew up in the country' and 'I'm a farm boy,' even a 'I paid my way through law school off a trapline.'"

"Something like your story."

"Hell, you know me; I'm just a little old country boy myself. I had a trapline when it was all I had in this world."

"All hands clasp onto their wallets . . . and back into a cor . . . ner," I chanted.

"Now, now, that ain't fair. . . ."

"Right, but what next?"

"Every country one of them said they was going home to get their knife and they'd be right back. Now I ask you, does a real farm or country boy even have to go home for his knife?"

"When they got back I suppose they just pitched right in?"

"Well, I wasn't too happy. Them beaver is spoke for in a good cause, and they got to be done right to bring top price."

"But eventually the old country boy made a deal with the farm boys, am I right?"

"Oh they talked me into it eventually. I'm letting them skin, fletch and stretch my beavers. . . ."

"And . . . ?"

"And they're all going to get up there and keep my roof shoveled next winter."

10

The Guv's Old Tackle Box

IT WAS LIMBO TIME IN MID-APRIL: FINALLY AND MERCIFULLY TOO late for ice fishing and too early for shooting gophers.

The gray, blustery Saturday was perfect for a man to spend in his garage hideout, a log or two charring in the airtight stove, savoring a little leftover chew from the hunting vest while finally cleaning rifles and shotguns from the fall season and replacing line and leader bird's nests woven by the memory of last season's monofilament.

Past seasons . . . Yes, it was still there, no need to look . . . right where it has been for . . . how many years now? . . . sealed and silent, that battered old tackle box, faithful companion of my father and me on hundreds of fishing trips. Is it really going on ten years since he died, since I have been unable to open that box?

There are good reasons not to open any tackle box in the spring, reasons that have to do with forgotten live bait and tangles, monofilament memory again, and Chinese puzzles with needle points and barbs. But with this tackle box, the reluctance had to do with knots of nostalgia, tangles of old memories and ultimately with the strong emotions that would be released immediately that lid swung open.

But on this day there was a reason to open the box. For Christmas there had been a tackle box like a semitrailer under the

66

tree, with tiers of drawers and trays, space enough to consolidate the contents of my two boxes and that of my son, John. My dad, the Guv, had collected lots of good stuff. Why shouldn't it join the family treasure trove? Holding my nose I dove in, snapped the catch and swung the lid back on the Guv's old tackle box.

There was really no need for the plugged nose, even if one of the first items in a top tray was a snelled hook, complete with worm. But the flesh was perfectly mummified, odorless. Otherwise, things were in an order unprecedented in our family. I recalled that the Guv died on May 16, opening day of the fishing season during my childhood, and the day it continued to open traditionally in our family long after official season openings and closings were abolished by law in Alberta. Could the old man, in his retirement, actually have had the leisure to get his tackle in order for once before his season started? If so, how to explain the worm? Or had he actually started his last season earlier than May 16? A man . . . his son . . . can only hope so.

First glance in the big bottom compartment had me grinning and nodding like a horse eating thistles. As he got older the Guv could stand the cold less and less well, so he bought this "beeper," for his bait fishing on the bottom. Basically it is an ordinary rod holder with a long spike, but this one has a button and horn that sounds when a fish is on and jerking. With that technology out there on the cold spring banks of Cowoki Lake, the old man could sit in the car, sipping tea and rocket fuel, the no-name, no-nonsense hospital brandy he favored, trading truths with a fishing buddy and waiting to hear the horn. His grandchildren will be amused with this find; I hope the Guv heard it beep a time or two in the six weeks or so before he died so suddenly.

Beside the beeper were the reels, and among them a long lost friend, my own first reel, a Bronson Fleetwing, level wind, that set me back $4.75 of my own money, new, in about 1950. A flick of the finger still spun the spool on to infinity, just as it did the day it convinced me to buy it. Avoiding backlashes with that reel kept my thumb honed to safecracker sensitivity. The Guv's old Shakespeare had probably long ago cranked its last, so he expropriated my old Bronson as insurance against spinning. He had converted to spinning, but he never fully trusted the Mitchell 300 ever since the day he used his first, much cheaper, spinning reel.

That was one hot day in the badlands when we were fishing our hole behind a rock reef in the Red Deer River. The Guv was initially delighted with spinning. His first cast sailed clear to the middle of the river. The bobber plunged as it floated around the end of the reef. Only after he struck the fish did the troubles start. What he had was a very large goldeye indeed, nineteen inches, my diary says, one inch under the then-current provincial record. But I swear that fish was halfway to the Saskatchewan border before the Guv could be convinced to stop cranking that spinning reel backwards. Such language as sounded and resounded, like the visible heat waves that afternoon, from those bare bentonite hillsides!

One thing about the old man: unless I was around to prod and push, he just would not use anything new unless he thought of it himself. There, in the top tray, was proof in gutta percha: a whole plague of exact imitation rubber grasshoppers, crickets, ants and so on that he once "sent away for" after seeing an ad, probably in one of my comic books. They disappointed him, of course; no fish ever took one, so he continued to believe there was no substitute for the real thing, and he ran down live grasshoppers long after he was so old and stiff he squeaked when he walked.

Proof of all that are the dozens of Le Tort Hoppers I had given him, there in the second tier, all of which he knew would catch fish. He had witnessed me and friends of mine taking many trout and goldeye on them. In fact, I believe the Guv did take fish with them on "my" water. Perhaps it was only on "his" water they would not work. Anyway, there they were in the tackle box, unused, along with those rubber "duckies," the imitation grasshoppers and crickets he had cursed so roundly but never discarded. One of the Guv's favorite lines was "You'll never know when it'll come in handy."

Also in that second tray were items to bring a tear and a smile. They were the things he never intended to use: the first Le Tort Hopper ever tied by his grandson and the second Despickable ever tied by his granddaughter (her first is somewhere in one of my fly boxes). The old pirate was a fish-eater who asked me many times to explain one more time my rationale for releasing big fish, but he would have starved before he ever risked using and losing either of those two flies.

But there! What's was that? In the third tray, full of well-used and still packaged jigs, my "sick canary" that I had considered long gone to wherever all lost lures go, a green-headed walleye jig with bright yellow feathers. The first time I ever tried it was the first time I ever tried any jig, and I took nine walleyes on nine casts. My friend Vern Caddy said it looked like a sick canary, but confiscated it, my rod, and took our tenth walleye on his first ever cast with a jig.

We retired that jig, undefeated, from active service for ten wrong reasons: the ten fish it had taken on ten consecutive casts. Now I know its real distinction is that it must be the only jig in the world to have survived ten casts without terminal snag and a trip to jig heaven. But suddenly, uncast, it had disappeared from my tackle box. Two more things about the Guv: he absolutely loved to eat walleyes, or pickerel as they called them down in his part of the country in those days, and he had a high regard for the veracity of Vern Caddy, they both being from the old country, as the Guv would say. Obviously inspired by Vern's tale, the old man borrowed the sick canary for a while, just to show John at the Marshall Wells store exactly what to order to slay the pickerel. John would immediately have recognized the genius of the jig from the tackle dealer's point of view and would have ordered thousands for his customers to decorate the rock and piling structure below the Bassano Dam on the Bow River.

Yet, in a compartment on the jig level were the "ice flies" and Russian hooks I gave the Guv, all still attached to their cards or in the plastic bags. The contradictions continued. Did no one he believed ever tell him that you really could take those Lake Newell "jumbo" whitefish through the ice on little jigs or Russian hooks? Even though I know he went to the grave convinced lake whitefish would not bite on anything, I believe the Guv never used those whitefish lures because he regarded ice fishing as a greater insanity than even moose hunting or releasing large fish. Where do I think I inherited *my* attitude to ice fishing, anyway? Come to think of it, where did I get the unmitigated insensitivity to give my father something for ice fishing anyway?

Now there was something I had forgotten about as completely as the day that sprang instantly to mind as I spotted the tiny, single hook, silver Gibbs spoon. It had to do with attendance at the opening ceremonies of the Kananaskis Highway and the catching in a beaver dam of a twenty-one inch cutthroat back in that wonderful, wild country we are now bent on turning into a resort for rich yuppie skiers and Japanese tourists. . . . But that is another story. . . . It took thirty-five years until last summer for me to surpass that cutt caught when I was maybe fourteen or fifteen. . . .

I close the box. This is all simply too good to do alone. On a wintry day, when the kids can help, is the proper time. Why did I wait ten years, I who know you can always tell a man by his tackle box? There is nothing in the Guv's tackle box but the spirit of a good man and hundreds of stories.

Alibis

11

Gunner's Alibi

T HE INSTANT CREATION OF ALIBIS TO EXCUSE SHOTS MISSED while hunting is a technique that escaped me until late in life. The reason was simple: from the start I got no practice; as a young lout, I never missed. But the story is how I gained wisdom, learned to appreciate, create and crave good gunner's alibis.

My first gun was a borrowed .410 double with hammers. In those days they believed it more important to shield a lad from recoil than to expose him to the possibility of hitting anything when he shot. Of course there was no such thing as practice, it being considered a mortal sin to expend a shotgun shell on anything that you could not eat.

On my first hunt my father placed me far off on the fringe of a pea field while he and the execution squad hid nearer to the decoys. Bathed in the golden glow of sundown, disoriented by the blockade he had just run, a Pintail drake in full fall plumage cruised straight for me in good range. He collapsed at my shot. My first duck with my very first shot, and I just could not believe it! I looked hither and yon, but eventually concluded it had to be me. Then the crushing responsibility of shooting alone engulfed me. From then on I, too, snuggled with the decoys, or at least the other hunters, and was able consistently to scream "I got one!" and it was always true. Those were bliss-

72

ful days: not only did I never miss, but it was a joy to see how my success pleased those natural deadeyes who hunted with my father. No jealousy there: they laughed a lot and seemed delighted every time I got another one.

Only one incident disturbed that truly happy first season. I was directed to block a wide, willow-choked ditch while Dad and our Labrador hunted it towards me. I snapped a shot through the willow at the fleeing wraith of a rooster. There was nothing to see and hear, particularly anything from me. But Buster presented me with a dead rooster when he and Dad arrived.

"Did you shoot?" I asked.

"Didn't," the old man replied. "You don't suppose it's possible to get a bird when nobody else shoots?"

Perhaps, but absolute truth was that if a whole bunch shoots, how is any member of it to know that any one person missed? I did not even philosophize on everyone missing because I was too busy slaving and saving. The old man had promised to match me dollar for dollar on a new double barrel 16-gauge. But when pay-up time came in the combined Bar and Gun Shop in Kalispell late the next summer, he made me pay the full shot! He would reimburse me later, surely, but all I ever got was an alibi for treachery.

"The gun did not cost as much as we expected. You have the money, and I don't. Besides, you will look after the gun better if getting it hurt a little."

Like most alibis, that one contained a grain of truth. I still have that Winchester Model 24, and it is in excellent condition. Although I have not shot it for ten years and have had offers for five times what the gun cost new, I cannot bear to part with it. The old man has been dead two decades, during which I have occasionally reflected that my first shotgun was a better one than he owned in all his life.

That gun and my Dad's old hunting buddy, Lee Metzger

of Santa Ana, California, taught me a couple of important lessons my second season. Metzger, another man who never missed, was in a slump. But he had only missed half a dozen in a row by the time I was free to take my new shotgun on a pheasant hunt. We surrounded a willow jungle on the edge of a leaky canal. Metzger and I were up on the bank on two corners. Dad, a friend and a couple of dogs were down below. A nice rooster screamed up in the middle of the bush.

"Good shot," Metzger said as the bird tumbled. "Thought I heard you shoot," I said.

"I did, too," Metzger said. "But when they get up now, I know I'm going to miss. Maybe I should see a shrink."

On an evening shoot a few days later, we set Metzger to blocking the ditch while the old man and I came down with Buster. The barrage started when we got halfway there. We saw Metzger break his slump: ten straight roosters without a miss.

"So, what's the secret?" the old man asked.

"That first one accidentally collided with my shot charge, and the rest of them did it on purpose."

When I finally finished ruining my eyes with seven years at university and law school I just wasn't swinging my 16 the way I used to when I was hunting nearly every day. In fact, I went into a fabulous slump wherein I missed thirty-nine straight pheasants over a three-season period. Worse than Metzger, I knew I would miss before a rooster got up. The sporting friend I call Baby Huey gave the alibi and the diagnosis:

"Pheasants got you psyched."

We tried everything except psychiatrists or practice, of course. During these times my friend Mac Johnston and I were trying out his Brittany, Plum, the first of any pointing breed either of us had owned. One day we rounded a corner of a tule patch, and there stood the ghostly statue of Plum in a clump of sweet clover.

"What the hell's he doing?" Mac asked.

"I do believe he's on point."

"Bull etcetera!" Mac said.

So I went by the book: crooned "whoa, whoa" at the dog and waded in clover with him. A big rooster flushed so close he tipped my cap, then crumpled at my shot.

"Nice shot," Mac said.

By then I was morbidly proud of my slump, suspecting a *Guinness Book* entry was within range of my errant shot patterns.

"The hell it was; I missed!" I screamed.

"No, I missed," Mac insisted. "That bird was flying too slow."

Now there was an alibi that damns with faint praise even as it shouts its own credibility. It is of a genre with the alibi ad-libbed every fall by shivering victims of moose fever who have just emptied a full magazine into orbit around the beast of their dreams: "That bull was too big." So I accepted that my greatest slump had been broken over the first point of Mac's Brittany.

Having moved further north, I had taken to hunting ruffed grouse. The old man came up and went out with us one day. He was astonished at the quick shots and the fact that I hit one occasionally. He diagnosed my pheasant shooting problem and proposed a long-term solution.

"Those ruffed neck grouse have ruint you. Now you are shooting at pheasants too quick," the old man said. "Why don't you try for pheasants with that sawed-off shotgun you are using on those queer grouse?"

Heresy! It would be me called queer. Down in pheasant country, real men shoot fully choked. But I took the advice and used my no-choke gun on pheasants. About this time, as well, my first really good pheasant dog shamed me into getting some practice at trap and skeet. Not only did my field shooting improve, so did the sophistication of my alibis.

Once during this stage I obtained a feather-light 12-gauge automatic with a short cylinder barrel. Its name was Deathwind, but only on the skeet range, where I could always be ready, finger on the safety button. So I relished the thought of the carnage in the pheasant fields. Never a feather did I touch! After a lifetime with the tang safeties of the doubles I favored, I never once got the trigger-guard safety off on that auto during the excitement of a flush of any creature not molded of clay. That first season I wore out two pair of gloves thumbing the tang shiny for the safety that was not there. But my companions grew bored with the obvious, excessive truth in that same old alibi, and I had to sell that gorgeous gun.

Many great alibis are stillborn, rendered redundant by a miraculous second shot. The longest shot I ever made with anything other than a typewriter is an example. That animal was so far away that I was folding up the bipod when I saw the pronghorn go down, then heard my bullet strike. My companions, a land surveyor and his party chief, paced the shot at 425 meters and were full of congratulations. But I was already wondering how I could rest the cross hair on the back line of the animal at that distance and hit him precisely there. Worse, why had I previously overshot the animal at a mere 100 meters? Alibi: 100 meters is too close for a real antelope hunter. But will the connection between the two shots ever be made, and does anyone really care after such a second shot? If you don't get caught, who needs an alibi?

The story of the finest black bear I ever missed illustrates the subtle difference between a reason and an alibi. After a long stalk down into the gorge of the Peace River a few years ago, we finally located the huge blond boar we'd seen from up top, sound asleep below us, not 100 yards away on a steep slope.

Only his head was completely exposed, but I did not wish to shoot such a trophy in the head. So I decided to aim right under his chin and slip the bullet into his chest. At the shot, the bear twirled like a top on his stomach, fully exposing his body broadside. You never shoot a bear just once, so I invited my companion, veteran Peace River bear hunter Don Norheim to finish the beast.

Following that shot, the orange flame of the running bear flickered through the dark woods.

"He'll drop," I said.

"Runs pretty good—for a dead bear," Norheim observed.

All I had done was kick sand in the bear's face. Norheim, too, had overcompensated for the steep angle of the shot. My analysis in retrospect, "There's no chest where I shot" is as true as it is lame. The alibi would be why I aimed where there was no chest, and that would be true too, but my lips are sealed. So are Norheim's. The secret comfort of each of us is that the other missed, too.

Mac Johnston is one of the greatest ruffed grouse shots I have ever seen. He is an exponent of the "edge" in grouse hunting. By this he does not mean hunting the edge of the cover, as the books advise, but the advantage "edgy" nerves provide in snapping off the quick shots necessary to hit ruffed grouse flushing and flying in thick cover. But one day he was missing everything. He would be the first to alibi that it was because he was too relaxed. When inevitably he found a grouse perched in a tree, he was so frustrated he shot at it. He missed the bird but severed its perch. Then the grouse flew and he missed again.

His son Iain, about twelve, caught up to the scene, full of indignation.

"Did you shoot at that one sitting in the tree?"

"Yes!" Mac roared, giving such a look, and taking half a step.

"Thought you would, but some days they just sit too still."

Such devoted sons are born masters of shooting alibis. Three years ago I got my first chance in some time at a double on pheasants. The right barrel connected, but the second rooster was unscathed.

"That second one was way harder," observed my loyal son.

Other times, the very best alibis afield, as in court, are frequently provided by third parties. My friend Hugh Landerkin was bemoaning to a friend the mystification he felt at cleanly missing an easy double on sharptails on a bitterly cold November day. This true friend was not mystified. At temperatures far below zero, he explained, the powder is far less efficient, pressures are lower and the shot charge has less velocity. Hugh had not, his friend explained, allowed for the chill factor. In this case, obviously, it was the chilled shot, not the grouse, that was flying too slow.

Got one!

12

Pheasant Fillosopher

HUNTERS AND FISHERMEN SEEM TO CHOOSE, AMONG THOSE professionals and tradesmen who work on them while they wait, like-minded outdoors people. My dentist, for example (we'll call him Dr. Moller), was chosen because he has superb dental skills, yes, but also because he is an ardent hunter, trapshooter and certified gun nut.

Dr. Moller had been seriously ill last year, and now we were playing checkup catch-up. Obviously there were fillings that needed replacing because my mouth was full of equipment, tools and material during my most recent visit, starting with mirror, fingers, drill and cotton "dams." As it turned out, Dr. Moller had some catching up to do, too.

"Doctor said I had to take it easy, get back into shape gradually," Moller said, "so I've been going to a pheasant hunting preserve. Ever been to one?"

"Unh uh."

"First time for me, too. Don't have to do nearly the walking you do after wild birds. Course, I kind of miss that walking.

"Come to think of it, There's lots of things you miss about real pheasant hunting when you hunt on a preserve. Organizing the group, eh? You know: somebody always cancels last minute; you have to find somebody else? Not down on the old pheasant farm. Get your reservation; they put out the birds. Hell, go by yourself if you want.

"No motel needed. No arriving in the dead of night and finding they've lost your reservation or let it go to a bunch of drunks from Calgary and you have to sleep in the car with the dogs. Why do I miss it though? On the preserve anymore, it's arrive at ten and depart at two with your birds.

"Remember all the eating out? On the wild hunts, doesn't one of the guys always get into too much wine and then fall into his soup. Or somebody else is grabbing the . . . uh . . . behind of the waitress, and it costs big bucks to quiet things down.

"So, one year you take a housekeeping unit. But one morning you ask for something to dung the doo out of the dog boxes, and your buddy hands you the spatula. Worse, he tells you to get it back quick, because he's got to turn the eggs."

"Aaghgll . . ."

"Better believe it, you miss a lot. All that give and take with the landowners, for instance. You remember: spending half the day hunting permission before you hunt pheasant *numero uno*.

"Then you line up a good place, hunt it and that night the farmer phones, mad as hell that you drove all over the fall rye he just irrigated. So then you spend to noon next morning going out and proving by the tire tracks it was someone else. That sort of thing. When you hunt on a pheasant preserve you miss all those good old human relations; just buy your birds, bag 'em and blast off.

"You know, those planted birds just don't run like the wild ones. First time down—eh?—old Red picked up and presented me with seven of my ten birds without ever a cap being snapped in anger. Sure as hell: if you have the dog, you don't need the gun. And vicey versey, too, of course.

"If I'm going to keep at it down there, it's dog or gun. Can't be both. But you know me. One of the things I just am not going to miss is hearing my own gun go off."

"Mmphh daawwk."

"You bet. But there's a million things I'm going to miss about the dog work alone. Ever stood around, shivering in the morning, while the dog hunches up a dozen times to get rid of the diarrhea from all that ditch water he's been drinking? Remember that?"

"Mmmpf."

"Sure you do, and you'd miss it too. Same as pulling the rose thorns out of your kneecaps every night, hosing the dust out of your eyes or hearing your buddy groan fit to die as he lowers his hulk into a hot tub after twenty-five miles on his pins for one wild pheasant.

"Wild? Remember how everybody, quote, 'limited out, and they was all wild birds,' unquote? Try that line down on the preserve and they'll revoke your membership.

"Now, without the dog you really miss a lot. For starters, except for the gunfire, the hunting is almost silent on those preserves. No whistles, no shouts. Hell, you almost forget how to swear.

"It's sort of lonesome, too, if you go alone: nobody to get the rabbit chasing done, nobody to climb up the diamond willow to pull the porcupines down, nobody to get between you and the skunks. You know, you arrive home from a preserve in mind and body fit to grope a waitress, but there's nobody around but Mother. Yes, that's something else you miss about hunting wild pheasants.

"Porcupines and skunks are nothing. It's the cow flops I really miss. You know: how a good dog picks only the vintage, I mean the greenest, the sloppiest cow flops to roll in?

"Of course you miss all of that on a pheasant hunting preserve. After all, they are farming pheasants, not cattle. Even if you needed a dog, there wouldn't be a flop for him to roll in, and that naturally leads to a whole bunch of good stuff you are just plain going to miss. Like finding a ditch full of scummy ice water for one thing, then trying to scrub the dog off with bare hands, using grass and mud for soap, and driving umpty miles home in zero degrees with all the windows open. . . ."

"Rougwk mumpff."

"Take it easy. Just a few minutes more now, and we'll be through.

"Tactics . . . planning . . . stragedy, as the fella says. Now that's something you really miss from hunting wild pheasants. You know, the birds should be in the tules because it's a stormy day? And don't forget to block the side ditches or they'll all run out on you?

"And the arguments? The new member of the group's been hunting pheasants exactly one day, but already he's telling you there's no pheasants in a prime patch you worked all morning just to get permission because there's no water. Or he explains to you exactly what it is your dog's doing wrong, never mind he's dead on his feet and stove up by cramps from three days of swamp water and hunting wild pheasants.

"Yep, it's tragedy how you miss the strategy, but down on the preserve you just don't need it. Hell, on a stormy day down there, you just follow the tracks of the stocking truck. The bird won't be ten feet from the last footprint of the person that planted him. Preserve birds stay planted!

"There. Now you can rinse. . . ."

"Damn you, Moller! I just laid out five hundred bucks for a couple dozen of those birds on a pheasant preserve to train my new Brittany!"

"Well, you may have to lay out that much again for one of these new canine psychologists to get him over the trauma when he discovers that real pheasants don't hold still. That is, of course, if you ever miss hunting wild pheasants enough to go back to it. . . . Cost. That's another thing. You know, I costed it out once, and I guess the thing I really miss most about hunting wild pheasants is paying a hundred bucks plus per pop for birds that no way are they steady to point or pounce. . . ."

"It's you, Moller, that I don't know if I'll get back to, ever again."

"Sure you will. Checkup in six months. You'll get a reminder in the mail. Always nice talking at you."

13

How to Eschew Snoose

WHILE REDISORGANIZING MY FISHING VEST RECENTLY, I found in an obscure pocket a crumpled foil pouch containing a couple of quids of chewing tobacco, and in another, one of those round tins of so-called smokeless tobacco, or as some he-men would call it, "spitless chew." It's a good thing neither came to light on those many occasions astream last summer, when I was dying for a chew. But now I was not even tempted and threw both packages into the trash barrel, thinking only a little bitterly of my antique, round-heeled, brass spittoon, a gift from my mother-in-law, now shined stainless, sitting forever still and silent on the hearth in the house, displaying Herself's bullrush collection.

A quiddity sang in my head of my first chew with my friend Grizzle Gutz Griffin. Griz christened himself, and he would whip any boy or girl, too, who called him "Augustus Maddox Griffin," as his mother preferred. We were being teased by Weasel Waugh, the clerk in the local general store, over our desire to buy a plug of Club chewing tobacco, alleged to be soaked in rum and dipped in molasses. Weasel was prepared to consider waiving the note from a parent but not the twenty-five cents cash, in advance.

We were saved by the arrival of Mr. Bunn, the local drayman, he of the vocabulary that, first blast, would remove paint and, even quoted second-hand, would prostrate mothers. We loved him. He was a positive inspiration to small boys, but, no, he could not see his way clear to advance us two bits against the next time we helped him deliver freight. It happened that he was in the market for a fresh plug himself, though, and he carefully pared a corner off that plug for each of us with his gorgeous staghorn Case knife, the one with only a little dried pheasant blood on the blade.

"Now," he said, "I want you to forget where you got this and remember that real men never spit."

Had we not been so anxious to get chewing we would have recognized this latter piece of advice as an outright lie. Outside our fathers, Mr. Bunn was the realest man any boy in town knew, and every boy who had hitched a ride behind Mr. Bunn on his horse-drawn wagon in summer or sleigh in winter needed only one time for it to soak in why you never stuck your head out to either side. The two hunting dogs that were always with Mr. Bunn did not even need one soaking.

After an eternity our gushers subsided to dry heaves and God in his mercy let us pass into a coma under the bridge where we had hidden to chew our Club. When I came to, I first thought Griz was dead. Then I thought they should use chew to teach kids multiplication. Griz's eyes looked like six holes burned in a bed sheet. Eventually the eyes simmered down to two holes, a little color seeped back into his face and my best friend spoke:

"We would never have survived two-bits worth."

From that first attempt we learned the benefits of moderation and the utility and beauty of spitting. We also learned that Mr. Bunn was even nicer than we thought: he lied just like any other kid. But it was to another, younger hero we turned, for an example, in the arts of expectoration. Our town had a superb

Junior B hockey team with an import goaltender from a town all of thirty miles away, "Snake" Woods, so named for anatomical reasons and because he had all the moves of a boa constrictor. He also chewed. The whole team dressed in a big room with one bare bulb hanging from a cord. If you watched carefully through the many cracks in the walls, you would see the goalie squint evilly up from lacing his skates: *"Ptsst." "Splat!"* Then the light bulb would be swaying and everyone under its dripping trajectory would be running for higher ground.

Unfortunately there came the tragic Sunday when Snake turned up at the rink with a mouth like a can of smashed raspberries and a package of soda straws through which he could draw sustenance until Doc Moller put his new store teeth together. This was in the days before the discovery of the slap shot forced Jacques Plante to invent the face mask. Saturday night Snake had taken a good wrist shot right in the gob, so deep that Doc Moller claimed he had to use blacksmith's tongs to amputate the puck. Sadly we small boys trooped out, knowing our hero's big league career was over, at least as far as spitting went, unless the dentist duplicated that magic gap in Snake's front teeth.

So we turned for instruction to the lobbies of the local hotels. But these were furnished with the hated, solid, respectable cuspidors squatting on flat bottoms. Toothless old men leaned over them and dripped like faucets. Not only was their tone flat as pewter, but these cuspidors did not rock to the tune of a direct hit like the sprightly brass spittoons furnished for the sporting types in the pool hall. Unfortunately the new owner of the pool hall was not an alcoholic, so was in no condition, as the former owner had been every evening, to let underage kids onto the premises.

But we persevered. We were the elite. We even recited a poem giving our opinion of kids who did not chew:

Rooty toot toot,
Rooty toot toot,
We are the boys from the Institute,
We don't smoke and we don't chew, (I think this was the word.)
And we don't go out,
With girls who do . . . ooh.
Our class won the Bible!

We never got sick again. Well maybe once, while we acquired immunity to the deadly Copenhagen, which was the only snoose available in those days. There were none of the candy arse flavors then (raspberry and wintergreen) and snoose-eaters were invariably quiet little guys who never seemed to say much or spit either. Now I know they could do neither, being comatose as opium addicts. To this day, whenever I slip a pinch of some sensational new flavored-snoose under my lip, a distant, angry whine starts in my head as though it were a wasps' nest, or a police siren mounted on the top of my spinal column. When I hear it I know I have sixty seconds to eject every particle of that deadly dust before I explode.

We had a couple of top sixteen-and-under baseball teams in town, and the genuine tobacco chewers scorned the players who merely faked the mandatory cheek bulge with Dubble Bubble. There is the story about the drunken duck hunter who, after killing his tenth straight lonely single flying over, explained it was impossible not to get at least one bird out of such big flocks. Multiplication again. But in baseball you have to catch the right one, and the kids who chewed only gum and thus saw only one ball at a time got the major league tryouts while the rest of us learned to write about chewing snoose and other sports.

The chewing habit stood me in good stead between college terms when I went to work on a gas pipeline where nobody could smoke. I still think fondly of lunchtimes on cold days with the warm quids steaming on the prairie wool like so many fresh horse apples. Conditioning in tobacco chewing also served me well when I decided to quit smoking forever, just about the time every outdoors magazine was full of ads wherein famous athletes urged we outdoors people to switch to smokeless tobacco. But I worry how the youth of today will ever acquire this useful skill.

Kindly mentors like Mr. Bunn are rare these days. But we do have instructive videotapes now on every aspect of the outdoors recreations. The best I have seen is *Lefty Kreh Chews!*, an eighteen-second production from load up to look out by Outdoor Skoals Productions. By all means, try chewing. You'll hate it, but don't give up: like all truly awful habits, it takes considerable willpower and dedication to acquire. Eventually you will even accomplish drinking beer and chewing at the same time. A tip: drink beer only from cans, and deposit the extract of tobacco from time to time in the empty. This obviates swallowing or expectorating on the floor, which prevents removal from the premises either in an ambulance or a paddy wagon. Use a blaze orange strike indicator from the old fishing vest to designate which can is the "hot" one. Try to remember. . . .

But perhaps I should not worry. How many times have I absolutely forbidden the louts in my life to touch my chew? Now they are in their late teens, and I find nephew Kurt carrying a pouch of Red Man in his fishing vest and son John confessing he was in the habit of swiping a quid of my Levi Garrett to pacify his mind on his paper route. Who says these modern kids are all bad?

So, how and why did I eschew (which is a marvelous old word, meaning *quit or shun something as wrong or distasteful*) snoose? One evening, just as I was having a Martini and contemplating linguini with clam sauce for dinner, Griz's eyeballs led him around the corner of my stump ranch porch. His eyes take him on a walk occasionally, when he feels the need to escape the trials of modern civilization whose name is Annie. He was enthralled with my recipe for ranch-style Martinis: wave a full glass of ice-cold Swedish vodka quickly in and out of the green sunlight shining through an empty, dry Vermouth bottle. Yes, he would try a Martini, and yes, he would stay for dinner. Among his trials he was in a quitting smoking mode and was sipping that Martini around a soother pellet of pure, refined and concentrated snoose (called, I believe, Oliver Twist) tucked behind his lower lip.

The genius of the pellet is that you can immediately eject every particle of that snoose in one pop as your ears give the first warning buzz. But Griz just accepted another Martini and went to the slope above the cabin to see if he could find some morels, those most delicious of wild mushrooms, for the clam sauce. He found two and celebrated with the deadly, poisonous third Martini. The clam sauce was so good that Griz may even have parked his pill. Certainly we had a glass of red wine or three as we ate. After dinner Griz tried a fourth Martini "to go" and another snoose pellet for dessert. Then we descended to the creek below the cabin to see if the salmon fly nymphs were emerging yet.

When I decided to return to the cabin the short way, up the face of the cliff, my friend followed. Halfway up there was an avalanche in which Griz was the principal ingredient. When the dust settled, there was Griz, miraculously unhurt, with his Martini unspilled. Without a word he picked himself up, chugged the Martini, staggered around the cliff, up the hill, then home. Next morning when I checked on him, he was stiff, sore, cursing and blaming that powerful little "suicide pill" of tobacco. The cynical tobacco chewer will even be heard to ask, "What about them morel mushrooms?" That, of course, emphasizes that Griz is either outright lying or has uttered a great truth. For an aging outdoor writer the "morel," perhaps, is this: trade truths rather than swapping lies, and strive always to avoid participating in avalanches. Personally, I believe old Griz, and so does he: Griz backslid to smoking and I have sworn a solemn oath to eschew chew forever.

14

Jigger's Elbow, Fly Tier's Finger and Other Outdoors Afflictions

D ID YOU EVER NOTICE THERE IS NEVER ANYTHING IN YOUR first aid kit or mentioned in its manual to deal with whatever the current crisis is? Check choking, for example, because doing that on camp grub is one of the hazards of outdoor life, according to an article, "Injury and Illness Among Deer Hunters" in the July 1989 issue of *Canadian Family Physician.*

They had to check choke in a hurry in one of those legendary camps along the Raven several years ago. One of the members suddenly turned purple and cross-eyed when a chunk of steak lodged crossways. I'm told you have three to four minutes flat to do something about this before death, maybe even something serious, ensues. My kit's manual says, "Thump victim on back; if a child, turn upside down while doing so." But this did not work with even a small pharmacist. The kit certainly did not contain those tong forceps thingies that are now standard issue, I am told, at better restaurants everywhere, the better to fish crossways grub out of cross-eyed customer's gullets.

Fortunately, on duty at this camp were at least one famed surgeon and a radiologist, neither of whom knew any more about Heimlich's famous maneuver than did their first aid kit's manual. So these specialists performed a tracheotomy with a filleting knife and tippet material. (Rapala knife and 3x tippet material, I believe it was, if you kids want to try this at home.) Neither of the doctors lacerated his left, or off-hand, which the *Canadian Family Physician* article says is the most frequent (nearly one-third) of all deer hunting accidents, presumably suffered during the gutting of deer, although shaving hair off one's forearm to prove the sharpness of one's knife the eve of the season opening has to figure in there somewhere.

A more common camp affliction is gastric upset, leading to what I call Camp Grub Flatulence. Apparently CGF cannot be cured, only controlled. The method is similar to that used to treat uncontrolled snorers: a supply of pup or mountain tents and banishment from the cabin, main tent or motorhome to the bush—way back in the bush. The cruelty of the cure is that the banishees will miss the world-class entertainment of listening to gents, exhausted from fresh air, exercise, camp grub and maybe even beverages, talking to each other in their sleep. I once yearned for a tape recorder as a renowned lawyer, a judge and a former judge argued an x-rated and absolutely hilarious case up in the sleeping loft.

Is there anything in the kits or manuals on how to treat a flinch? No, not your shooter's flinch. I mean Product Liability Warning Flinch, of which I suffer a major dose, having made a recent trip on a quad ATV and also having purchased a new freestanding, elevated deer stand. Those two wonders of modern technology are responsible, according to statistics, for an epidemic of injury and death to outdoors persons. The new Kamikaze 500 I was riding need not have been painted at all, so plastered was it with warning decals about being under sixteen, doubling up and all manner of hazards to which no loving, indulgent modern parent pays the slightest attention. Incidentally, does that recent case where a hunter blew away both his buddies off one quad with one shot not rest our case on doubling up?

Every second line of the six-page assembly instructions for the tripod deer stand was a blaze-orange death threat; for example: "You have just purchased a product which, if not used and maintained correctly, could cause you to be permanently seriously injured or even killed." Particularly cunning is the skull and crossbones burned into the platform floor, right where it will stare you in the eye as you climb up or jerk awake from the deadly stand-snooze. Yes, this stuff is dangerous and can cause serious injury, even death, all right, particularly if you dwell morbidly on those warnings and flinch at the wrong time, such as while getting in or out of the bathtub.

What about the terminal wader rash caused by spending a third of each year in the old Royal Red Balls or other makes of chest waders? There is a diagnosis problem here because the bandy-legged, saddlesore slouch of the sufferer is identical to that of a victim of *Mal de Raquette*, which is not, as you might translate, tennis elbow but snowshoer's affliction, the excruciating pain in the balls (of the foot) from snowshoeing too long and far, but which any sufferer can tell you actually extends much farther north, yea even unto the old royals.

Accurate diagnosis is important because the method of treatment is very different for each malady. There is some small comfort in surveys which show that almost half of all medical general practitioners can distinguish winter from summer approximately half the time and might thus distinguish between wader rash and *Mal de Raquette*, unless, of course, the victim is one of those nuts who dons the waders and snowshoes to shuffle into some premature spring fishing. The survey had 998 respondents, which gives it a margin of error of plus or minus 5.2 percent nineteen times out of twenty, but the margin of error increases to 11.1 percent if just two specialists are added to the sample.

Four or five years ago bad weather delayed the fly-fishing

season into mid-July. Then suddenly there was an all-day Pale Morning Dun hatch that, out of shape as I was, I flogged steadily away at for twelve glorious hours. Next day I could not lift a #20 PMD imitation with my right hand or do the twisting to tie it on the leader with a clinch knot without screaming in agony.

"Have you had this before?" my personal general practitioner asked.

"Couple days."

"Well, you still got it."

He referred me to a renowned physiotherapist who told me I had tendonitis of the elbow, or tennis elbow, or angler's elbow. About this same time, my old friend Bob Jones, then president of the Outdoor Writers of Canada, wrote a column describing as "jigger's elbow" what he was then suffering in both arms and agonized that striking a fish crossed his eyes and dotted . . . er, buckled . . . his knees. One wag suggested he should just jig with a different squid, but Jones said he was not up to that. But surely we digress.

My physiotherapist reminisced that on his final exam in England he was asked to list twelve methods of treatment of tennis elbow. "The bad news," he said, "is that means any or none of the twelve might work." Over half a year we tried most of them, leaving only cortisone, acupuncture and surgery. I rejected acupuncture on the basis of the second opinion of my dog's veterinarian that "the theory of yin and yang is out to lunch acupuncture-wise." So I selected the deadly cortisone shot into the joint. When the anesthetic wore off I took to my bed, mewling and puking like Shakespeare's infant, in agony for an entire gorgeous long weekend. But that terrified the wonky joint into remission where I have kept it since with an early spring stretching and strengthening program with "squeezers," dumbbells, the world's finest collection of forearm straps around the shift lever of my fishing rig and perhaps the only known prescription for nothing heavier than four-weight fly rods. . . .

"Me! Me! What about me?" suddenly whines the little voice of Luke, my famous finger, index, left hand. The tip joint on this one has long been gnarled, the result of having caught in my youth on too many ball teams for too many wild farm boys. Suddenly, as middle-age stalked me, the nail turned chalky white.

"Have you had this before?" my G.P. asked.

"Never."

"Well, you sure got it now," he diagnosed.

He put me out on waivers to a dermatologist and advised me to photograph the finger with my macro equipment in case the condition cured itself before my appointment next century or so. Diagnosis? "Leukonychia," *Dorland's Illustrated Medical Dictionary* informed me, is what I already knew: "a whitish discoloration of the nails of unknown cause." Dull. Mundane. So was the treatment: coated aspirin.

Then my G.P. sent me a copy of the August/September 1990 issue of *The Canadian Journal of Dermatology*, directing my attention to a "Case Report" on page sixty-seven written by my own dermatologist, complete with one of my own shots of my own finger (but no credit line for my photograph) and three x-rays of somebody's first index finger joint.

The doctor shared with his readers much more than I had told him or he me: Leukonychia can be congenital or acquired, and mine was obviously acquired, he wrote, from the constant low-level pressure of spending "a minimum of four hours a day mounting and designing his own flies. Instead of using a vise to hold the materials, the patient holds the hook firmly between the left thumb and index finger."

No, Dave Berry, I am not making this up, but the specialist can answer to his own spiritual advisor. The fact is that spending more than fifteen minutes of any day tying flies gives me a bad dose of Camp Grub Flatulence. Where had Derm Doc got this stuff? I accused old Luke, my fickle finger. That dastardly digit trembled, broke out in a cold sweat and our nail went even whiter. Bitterly I recalled yet another line from Shakespeare: "No man's pie is freed from his ambitious finger."

No question I have tied thousands of flies, at the rate of three per day during the winter which takes, max, fifteen minutes per day. Of all those, I have tied exactly two in my bare hands, one while being instructed by the late great Lee Wulff himself. My dermatologist may have missed a calling as an outdoors writer when it comes to never to allowing the facts to obstruct a good story.

He did get one more shot at it and my famous finger got even more press when an alert reader of *Fly Rod & Reel* (probably a fly-fishing dermatologist) sent in the medical article and they ran a bit on it in their "Short Casts" column, giving a name in their headline to this new malady and more fame to the only finger ever to suffer it: "Fly Tier's Finger." Our mutual nail turned pink and shiny when I told Luke we were going to separate and that modern freeze-dry taxidermy would make it possible for him perpetually to "give the finger," mounted on a pedestal either in the Museum of Fly Fishing in West Yellowstone or the Canadian Medical Hall of Fame, if there is such a place.

There are worse afflictions, far worse, than strange, undiagnosable maladies, even imaginary new ones, or even those with a dozen or more noncures. They are called tests. Four or five years ago I came down with the mother of all doses of world-class CGF from a camp in Montana by way of Baja. Anyway, we trotted on and on from the end of the hunting season nigh unto the start of fishing. How many times did my family physician say to me "Have you had this before?"

"Months and months. . . . Gangway!"

"Well, you sure still got it."

Eventually he sent me to a specialist in internal medicine who wrote out orders for tests at the hospital. The first involved a Sigmoidoscope, a device like a plumber's snake, only with eyes. I swear it is thirty-five feet long, but what it is intended to slither along and eyeball is only thirty-two feet long. Actually, in retrospect of what was coming, this one wasn't too bad, except when Doc drove her into the curb a time or three there, going around corners.

But the next, an Air Contrast Barium Enema, I believe it was called, involved a bung with a hose through it, a spray paint compressor and an x-ray machine capable of putting a body in positions only dreamed of even in pornographic videos.

A hint of what was to come came at sign-up time of such an impressive batch of releases and legal liability waivers that it brought on a dose of Product Liability Warning Flinch.

"Have we had this test before?" asked the sweet young x-ray technician.

"Don't know about you, but me . . . maybe . . . years ago . . . can't remember."

"I'll put you down for a no," she said. "If you ever had this one before, you'd never forget it."

15

Bonasa Days—Grousing in Paradise

EVERY LIE IN THE LITERATURE OF GROUSE HUNTING CAME TRUE one day fifteen years ago when I shot fourteen ruffed grouse, including a couple of doubles, and one retarded, reloaded triple. In several instances the dog flushed another grouse as he was retrieving the most recently demised. Much of it was simply being in the right place at the right time, but the major explanation is that we were in the high point of the cursed northern ruffed grouse cycle, what I like to call Bonasa Days. I pray never to have such a day again.

The "down-easter" will not understand this point of view. To many it will seem to be grousing in paradise. They will yearn for their own Bonasa Days. The best I can do is assign some reading. Remember the beguiling story by G.E.M. Skues called "Well I'm D. . ."? The gent dies and finds himself in a place where he catches a good brown trout on the first cast, another in the same place on the next and begins to feel at home in heaven. When he finds he must go on catching that same fish, without rest, forever, he begins to understand he has misjudged his location, and so should the envious down-east grouse hunter.

At least part of my poor attitude comes from shattered illusions, the yawning chasm between the dream and the reality. Some day someone will do a study on the brain damage suffered by those of us who grew up during and just after the last world war on a steady diet of the "big three" outdoors magazines. I was a prairie boy, living in Brooks, Alberta. My dad's best hunting buddy was rich, had subscriptions and gave us all his old sporting magazines, which I devoured and hoarded. Gradually, in those magic pages, I learned to accept the inferiority of our pheasant, notwithstanding that hundreds of rich and famous Americans would take over our town every fall to participate in what was then regarded as the best pheasant hunting in North America. The "King of the Game Birds," I grew to understand and accept, without ever having seen one, was the ruffed grouse, and I cherished that illusion until considerably after I was twenty-five and had moved north in my western province to an area which was submarginal pheasant habitat, but which was the home of the king.

Fate placed me in the hands of my long-time law partner, Mac Johnston, who had grown up in Prince Edward Island and who carried an Ithaca double 12-gauge that had been custom-built for his grandfather's ruffed grouse hunting. That gun, as I discovered, had more spread than a peanut butter factory, so much so, that Mac had to be careful not to take too wide a stance when he shot, lest he lose a toe or, worse, puncture his beloved Bean's Maine hunting shoes. The reason for the spread was not immediately apparent, as Mac's first stories about the gun were of the day a small boy saw his grandfather stop the horse and wagon and ground sluice a grouse on the road ahead, and of the time Mac, himself, big enough then to lift the Ithaca, sluiced a whole covey of Hungarian partridge down a "turnip drill."

Prophetic though these stories have turned out to be, I did not believe them at first because they contradicted the holy writ on down east "patridge" hunting as set out in the big three; besides, I had not yet hunted ruffed grouse and learned that even royalty can be just plain folks when in another kingdom. That first season all I did was hunt them. Mac didn't see the first ruffed grouse I ever saw, but he dropped it behind him anyway, or so it seemed to me, by shooting in front of him with that marvelous Ithaca. Then I understood spread.

"We're not going in there!" was my most frequent comment that first season as Mac would lead me into cover dense enough to give a snake the bends, where we would hunt a bird that went up like thunder and was behind a bush or tree before you could decide whether to have a heart attack or a nervous breakdown instead. We were hunting without dogs in those days and found infallible flushing ploys to be getting engrossed in lighting a cheroot or relieving one's water pressure. Some of the more spectacular shots in outdoor sports have been made when grouse have exploded during such operations, particularly the latter. Unfortunately today's outdoors magazines are too serious to publish such pictures. But I digress. That first season I did not fire a shot. All I got was a sunburn (on the roof of my mouth) as I waited vainly for the fool things to top the bush like a pheasant does.

"They don't," Mac said. "You have to get a shot off, fast. You got to have the edge." I soon learned he did not mean "hunt the edge," as the big three were always advising. He meant maintaining season-long edgy nerves so you attacked the thunder, cleared brush with the first barrel, then grassed grouse with the second. I began to suspect then, and know now, that Mac is probably the greatest grouse shot I will ever see. Under his tutelage I at least got some shots off the second season, but hit nothing but fresh air, brush and ultimately the ground.

It was when I started to look for a grouse gun to use instead of my double 16, bored full and modified, that I began to learn something about the king and hunting him in the northwest. Without even thinking about it, the first dealer handed me an over and under .22 rifle and .410 shotgun. "That's what everyone is using to get a mess of these new chickens that's been turning up in the woods lately." Believe it or not, our northwest grouse cycle is so extreme that some people forget the species even exists in the busts between booms. When populations build to a new boom, the popular lore is that we have a new product of evolution or creation of the Almighty, depending on theological stance of whatever damn fool is spouting this nonsense.

On this frontier, grouse hunting is not regarded as a sport, but rather as a substitute for a trip to the poultry counter. The .22 barrel is used first to pot the bird off the ground or a limb. The popular name for the King in our parts is bush partridge or fool hen, and in the unlikely event it even bothers flying, if you miss that first head shot with the rifle, you will waste the cheapest shell possible with the .410 barrel at a flying target everyone knows is impossible to hit. Shocked, I rejected the detested rifle/shotgun and eventually found a secondhand Ithaca side by side 12-gauge and bribed a gunsmith to hack and hone it into a clone of Mac's grandfather's gun.

Mac and I remained determined to hunt the King exclusively in the down-east fashion of his most loyal subjects. We bought new gentlemen's togs until we looked like we had oozed off a page of an Orvis catalogue. Mac acquired a Brittany, Plum, coincidentally, as I found later, the same unusual name borne by a Brittany once owned by Leigh Perkins, president of Orvis.

The season is traditionally more than three months long out here, and before that one was half over, the gentlemen's togs were shredded to mattress ticking and Plum had suffered most of the brain damage that was to afflict him for the rest of his life. Ruffed grouse are just too nervous for most pointing dogs to hunt and stay sane.

When you hunt ruffed grouse with a pointing dog in the northwest, you are employing an inferior version of his most efficient predator, the coyote. Fool Hens are evolution's product: coyote survivors. Our Ruff tiptoes away from the staunchest points, then jumps into trees, posing proudly, only to become higher fodder for goshawks and great horned owls. From the only productive points I have ever seen on ruffed grouse, the birds inevitably are flushed by the hunter far out of range of the unchoked blunderbusses we sporting ruffed grouse hunters carry. It evolves here that a pointing dog quickly regresses to coyote, tries to catch the bird, then learns to bark "treed." Which, of course, leaves the hunter to consider personal evolution, or a reversion, at least to develop a policy in this chess game for when the King "castles" in trees. In this, as in all matters of grouse lore, Mac was my guide and mentor.

Mac's policy was that we would faithfully do everything he could think of for three minutes flat to make the bird fly: shake the tree if it was small enough or throw rocks, clods or limbs. But when, as usual, nothing worked, Mac would order me to dispatch the grouse with apologies and alibis "to improve the breed," or "if God didn't intend them to be potted, he wouldn't've made them taste so good." I suppose you could say that if we dispatched enough of them, only those that hold steady to a point and flush would be left, and then we could buy some new togs and dogs and hunt the King as his gentlemen subjects should.

But the task, at the top of the cycle, seems impossible. There are birds everywhere: in bunches, incomers and outgoers, right to lefts and left to rights, bumping into each other and scaring men and dogs until you would swear there was yet another air traffic controllers' strike. As the numbers increase, just as is the case with overpopulating humans, the ruffed grouse becomes more and more foolish and stupid. What is so remarkable about the fourteen-grouse day I had is not that I got so many but that I got them all flying. For a long time after that, I lived in mortal terror that I had killed the last fourteen grouse in the kingdom possessing the genes for flushing and flying.

Recent years have put my fears to rest. We have gone from Bonasa to bust. As they get scarce, the birds flush wilder and wilder. In lean times it would seem easy to extirpate the tree-ing birds, except that I have been trying in vain for five years with two dogs to get one picture of a partridge in a tree. But I do not get discouraged. All true grouse hunters are like the gent the prospective bride described as she explained why she needed forty-two yards of filmy material for her one bridal negligee: "He would rather hunt for things than find them."

The hunting lately has approached the magnificent, down-east experiences I read of as a kid, where you can bust brush for twenty miles and have a great day if rewarded only by the sound of a couple of Kings flushing fine and far off. The reason they get all that consistent quality hunting down east, I expect, is that they are never plagued with the Bonasa Days as we are. In the northwest we are doomed by the boom to enjoy that quality hunting afforded by the mere memory of the King of the game birds for only a short period every ten years or so.

Two years ago the hunting got so good I never even heard a grouse flush, and I had to send my new pup to camp so the trainer could show him what a game bird is. But in Nature all good things come to an end. Several times while still hunting deer this past season I suffered both nervous breakdowns and heart attacks when ruffed grouse exploded beside or behind me. Then my friend, the legendary Baby Huey, nonchalantly took a double on flying grouse with one shot. But dread and foreboding really overtook me the other day as I watched a country purveyor of hardware unpack a crate of rifle/shotgun over/unders. "Oughta get yourself one of these beauties," he said, "instead of that old Parker you lug around. The boys say they are plumb poison on these here new ruffed neck grouse that has been turning up everywhere from here to the correction line."

16

Miracle Moose and
Mal Demise

THE MIRACLE, AS ALWAYS, WILL COME LATER. BUT "MISE" COMES from one of the more famous moose stories, "The Plural of Moose is Mise," written around 1921. It has occurred to me since I first read the story in the midfifties that it told little truth about moose hunting as practiced in my country, by Canadians, from coast to coast.

There is a fever, call it Mal Demise, that ravages many Canadian adolescents between the ages of eight and eighty unless they catch it earlier or live longer. The cause may be found in our recent history. There are still many gents of middling age who grew up on stump ranches here and there, where the moose was beans and buffalo to their tribe, most of whom now live closer to the supermarket than the swamp. These old boys still feel their hackles rise at the mere rumor of moose.

How bad it can get is illustrated by one of my first hunts with a former northern Saskatchewan boy. I took a game trail around the upwind end of a little swamp, hoping to push a deer across the opening he was watching. When I emerged, my friend was suffering moose malaria: he was broken out in a cold sweat, trembling, eyes bugged and glassy. The reason? I had pushed a cow moose by him and only bulls were legal. He was so delirious he even confessed he carried a moose tag, an absolutely forbidden act in my camp or company.

"Tell me about your unhappy childhood," I soothed.

"I grew up on a stump ranch in northern Saskatchewan," he said, "and like all the kids around, I ran a trapline. From some of the proceeds, I bought a .303 Enfield and spent the couple of years I had to wait until I was legal whittling, honing and filing, customizing that rifle."

An old, familiar Canadian story. I nodded encouragingly.

"Up there," he went on, "after the farming and before the winter sawing, there was moose hunting. Everyone got together to lay in some meat for winter. Finally came the day when I could go. My old man ran me up a tree at the neck of a swamp, placed some other standers, then the rest of the neighbors went to drive the swamp. Suddenly there were moose everywhere. I shot nine of them."

"Nine!"

"This was a communal hunt, remember. For food. The old man didn't even have to tell the other standers to shoot every one they saw. . . . When they all showed up, Dad strutted around among five tons of dead meat like a dwarf in the Black Mountains."

"I'll bet he was proud."

"You've got to know the old man. What he said was: 'Not bad, son, but there was eleven in that bunch.'"

Fortunately I escaped the Mal Demise virus. I grew up on the desert where formerly the buffalo roam'd, where the antelope and the lesser members of the deer family still play'd, and never was heard a discouraging word of moose or moose hunting. Eventually I moved to the swamps and sandhills of Central Alberta, where, although I personally did not have a moose tag, I was prevailed upon a time or two, in all innocence, to assist in the field dressing and removal to a proper place of internment of a moose or three that someone else had shot. The hard facts immunized me against a disease to which I had formerly been exposed only in romantic legends and literature. There is no question in my mind that hunting the wily bull moose can be challenging and beguiling, and that partaking of his flesh can be at least a sustaining and often a gourmet experience, but what happens in between is generally a human experience of the kind that should be condemned by Amnesty International. Nothing ruins a good moose hunt like getting a moose; then the fun is over for all concerned except the moose, which is mercifully dead.

Another hunting companion at age fifty regarded it as disgraceful that any Canadian good old boy should not have taken at least one moose. So, first he bought the tag, then he discovered that nobody would go with him. He went anyway, alone, and about 10:00 A.M. shot a bull that wandered even deeper into a red willow jungle before dying. There was no snow and it was so thick in there that he could not just backpack the quarters out, one at a time, the mile and a half to his truck. That way he would have had to be satisfied with the one quarter because he would never again have located the rest. So he leap-moosed, quarter by quarter for short distances, loading his packboard, unloading and reloading interminably. At 6:00 P.M., when he phoned me, his voice sounded like a north wind soughing through an old folks' home.

Instead of learning his lesson, he became addicted to the succulent flesh of moose. A year or two later, he was surprised by the opening of the season when all he had sighted in was a Savage 99 in .250–3000 for the 90-grain hollowpoints he had been using all summer to control gophers on his farm. At sunup a choice spike bull stuck his head out the near side of the swamp. He happened to have a moose tag because his lodge wanted a moose for their annual game banquet. The little bullet zipped between two ribs and the bull collapsed, as though all his strings to heaven had been cut, right where a utility trailer could be backed to his nose. This beast is forever known in local lore as the "Miracle Moose of the Mystic Shrine"; moose that can be removed from bog to butcher, hulk to hamburger, without hernias all around are miracles, the rarest game there is.

It is axiomatic: a moose, perfectly hit, dead on its feet, is, like the archetypal wronged spouse, the last to know. Invariably the beast wanders off over 500 meters of impenetrable deadfall, or half a kilometer of bottomless muskeg before dying. A local minister once road hunted and shot what he prayed was a miracle moose, but the dead beast then wandered to his last repose the mandatory 500 meters over the giant's tinker toy tangle of deadfall left in the wake of a tornado. The fabled solution for this problem is to camp by the carcass, burning all that firewood and eating moose meat until either the beast is totally consumed or a path is cut to drag the remainder to the vehicle. But the next vehicle up the road was a Nodwell, a tracked vehicle with a winch and miles of cable. It is miraculous how a moose will winch for miles over deadfall. But this was not an authentic miracle moose. Nor is whatever it turned out to be available to the average man without the powers of the cloth.

While his companions were praising his everlasting Reverential self, his ineffable, unerring marksmanship and the Lord and Savior in their own profane fashion, the Reverend was quietly praying for deliverance. The moose was your standard ghost walker: the Nodwell was the miracle.

The stories of outrageous misses are a moose-hunting cliché. A young outdoor writer recently regaled me tearfully about how he missed a moose with all five shots, broadside, at no more than 100 meters. Typical: nobody ever misses a long shot at a moose. Bull fever? Not on your life. A dose of reality suddenly breaks their fever, cures their Mal Demise: suddenly they see up close how big the problem is if they shoot the bull, so they miss the whole magazine on purpose. "That moose stood too still," they say, or "That one was too big!"

Treason though it may be for a Canadian, I am proud to admit I have never personally owned a moose tag, nor knowingly hunted with anyone having one in his possession. Well once, maybe, and not just because the metal detector at my deer camp failed, either. No, it was a subsistence case; worse, a hardship case. Russell Thornberry, who had just given up the real world for full-time outdoor writing and guiding, thought a moose in the freezer would be good insurance against famine. Did I know of a likely tree for a moose stand? Sure I did. Russell, after all, is a Texan, and Americans seem strangely immune to Mal Demise. So I helped a moose of a man put his platform up the aspen I selected. The stand overlooked a crossing of two good game trails deep down in a creek bottom.

"Uh . . . How do you get an animal out of this hole?" Russ asked.

"Last one I got, I floated down the creek. . . ."

"Oh."

I did not tell the lad that one was a smallish mule deer buck. What I said was: "If it's a moose, don't call us, we'll call you."

Next morning it was pouring. Out we went anyway. At midmorning tea we all agreed we had heard a shot, and elementary triangulation indicated it had to have been Thornberry. His vehicle was gone when I went to check. The windows of the cabin were all fogged when we arrived. Thornberry was inside, airtight stove humming, stripped to his steaming skivvies, drinking tea.

"Who'll help load a moose?" he asked.

"Oh, hell!" we all shouted.

He had been up the stand for all of five minutes when a fryer bull strolled along. Russell dressed the beast himself. He could not drag it, but did jerk it 100 meters to the bank and let it slide into the river, where it didn't float proudly like a small mule deer at all. No, it emitted two great bubbles, then sank like a Mafia corpse. By brute strength and some vestigial buoyancy, Russ wrestled the carcass down to the corner of the hayfield where he tethered it in a deep pool to a fence post. After lunch, in bright sunshine, we went down and I winched the moose, like a prehistoric monster from the primordial soup, up and into the hayfield.

Present were several lads whom I have previously suspected of harboring moose tags. Before I winched the bull into the utility trailer, I challenged any of the assembled multitude, or any combination of them, excluding Thornberry, to budge that carcass one inch. They all just stood, eyes glazed, with moose eating grins on their faces.

"Let that be a lesson to you," I snorted.

But it won't. They were all old Canadian boys, after all, with a fresh booster shot of Mal Demise virus infecting their bloodstreams. What is to be done?

Hair-trigger thinkers assert that the answer to moose hunting's greatest drawback has to be calling: luring Mr. Moose to a convenient location and executing him there. Thus does a whole shameful subculture thrive. Devices are manufactured: honey pails with shoestrings, stroked and plucked by virtuosos with all the talents of the legendary Manitas de Plata; birchbark horns sold everywhere, even to innocent tourists and children. During the rut, from coast to coast (half an hour later in Newfoundland), every Canadian bog and swamp resounds with raunchier bawls, bellows and grunts than one is likely to hear in all the massage parlors of the nation put together. There are even callers of such low cunning and mind that they will use a birch-bark horn to scoop up some water and pour it out in the manner, they suppose, of a "cow a—peein'." Even I have acquired consummate calling skills, but just to learn for sure where the moose are and get the hell out of there.

Yes, moose calling attracts moose. Too well, apparently, according to story after story in the hook and bullet press. You have never known the experience of being torn and tossed by cosmic forces in a black hole until you have been run over by a moose. You do not know cuts, scrapes, contusions, abrasions and outright fear until you have abandoned your rifle and been run up a swamp spruce by a red-eyed bull belching steam and halitosis, who then strives to uproot the tree with those dozer blades he carries aside each earhole.

Obviously the danger is a drawback to calling. The responding bulls are frequently enraged, allegedly because their prurient hopes have been so aroused by the calling, then so summarily dashed upon arrival at the source of the deception. But I do not believe that for a minute. No, my theory is that the moose responding to the call is merely outraged by all that human bellowing and bawling of obscene language in what was formerly a nice, quiet, Christian swamp.

In addition to being dangerous, calling is no real solution to the utter torture of moose hunting. There has to be a swamp or jungle of blowdown within moose hearing distance, otherwise there will be no moose to hear. No matter that you summon Mr. Moose to the intersection of Yonge and Bloor in bluest Toronto (a good calling location: the wind is in your face wherever you turn) and make a killing shot right there, he will be back in the middle of his muskeg or timber tangle before he surrenders his immortal soul. In fact, it is arguable that the called moose will go even further on his death stroll simply because he is so angry and full of adrenaline.

Modern science has yet to develop a cure for Mal Demise. There is only the hope that the disease might be controlled while research goes on. Years ago, as a public service, I founded a group called Algoholics Unanimous, the name being a tribute to the reputation and methods of another great organization and to the fact that the national sport and scourge of Sweden is hunting Algs, which is what they call moose. Our method? Whenever you feel a binge of moose hunting coming on, just phone another member: he'll invite you over to get drunk instead.

17

Getting Found Out

Iᴛ ʙᴇᴄᴀᴍᴇ ᴏʙᴠɪᴏᴜs ʟᴀsᴛ ғᴀʟʟ ᴛʜᴀᴛ ғᴀʀ ᴛᴏᴏ ᴍᴀɴʏ ʜᴜɴᴛᴇʀs were getting found out in my neck of the woods. At last count, just before the season closed, twenty-two souls or so had been found out there. Most protested they were not lost, as the finders dragged them, kicking and screaming, into hospitals for observation. These days it seems impossible for a self-respecting hunter to get and stay lost for any reasonable length of time.

I have read the newspaper accounts about the found-outs, and have interviewed one or two in my day. Slowly, impertinent questions have formed in my mind: Could it be that getting found out was all their own fault? Could they have stayed lost if they had really tried? Where did they first go astray? What did they do wrong?

Certainly they were easy finds for a helicopter. Almost to a man (this is not sexist; women simply are not as interested in getting lost as men), the found-outs were wearing blaze orange or scarlet. They had refused to splurge on a camouflage outfit, the sort now legal in most provinces.

"Try to save a little money by wearing out the old, bright overalls," one of them bitterly observed, "and look what happens."

Far worse, many of the found-outs were riding shiny new trikes in flashy colors that glared fit to blind the spotters in the helicopters. Many of these sportsmen had traveled exclusively on seismograph or logging cutlines through the bush, which is bad for at least three reasons. First, it is a simple matter for a helicopter to follow ATV tracks on a cutline. Second and third, the combination of cutlines and ATVs encourages weak people to penetrate too far into the wilderness and too far is precisely the first place searchers will look. A man who wears blaze orange overalls and rides a yellow Hiroshima Bomb on an open cutline is begging to be found.

Most of the found-outs admitted they had no compass, no aerial photograph and no topographical map. No doubt, they figured, such omissions would help them get lost and stay lost. Wrong! Stupid! A compass, photos and topos are absolutely essential if you want to find truly impenetrable wilderness where nobody can find you. They can even help you find the perfect place: one so close, so obvious, that search and rescue would never dream of looking there.

The protests of all last fall's found-outs reminded me of a legendary wandering mountain man who was once asked if he had ever been lost.

"Hell, no," he replied, "but there was a three-week period once where I was in considerable doubt where found was." Bragging? Perhaps. But such an achievement does take considerable talent and planning. Lost for three weeks! Obviously there was no busybody to call down the helicopters; clearly there was not a soul who knew even that he was going, let alone where he had gone.

Panic must be conquered, but not for the reasons given in those righteous survival manuals. The fact is that fear of getting and staying lost is simply the prime cause of getting found. Not so long ago I had the opportunity to spend a few days hunting with the Perfesser, a gent who seemed a contradiction in terms: he warned me that, notwithstanding his terror of getting lost, he had a habit of doing just that. Now, that presented a problem because he died to get his first ridge-running trophy mule deer buck. To do that you have to get up on the ridge, run with them and learn that time and direction simply mean nothing to these magnificent beasts.

So, first night in camp, while I prepared dinner, I sat the Perfesser down with compass, aerial photos and topographic maps. He could not even get them right side up! When I turned from peeling an onion, there he sat—stiff, glassy-eyed, trembling, a classic case of agoraphobia, or whatever. He was lost already, on paper and in my cabin! All my audio visual aids had done was paralyze the Perfesser with fear of getting lost in the vast wilderness portrayed there for him on paper. How could such a person, I wondered, ever avoid being found?

It turned out he couldn't. Out on those ridges he would not let me out of his sight. Whenever I turned around, there was the Perfesser, found. But so was I! That is what is so insidious about the fear and panic of only one person: it can cause even innocent bystanders to get found, too. Suffice it to say I was a nervous wreck, and the only creatures to remain unfound were those monstrous, ridge-running mule bucks.

Strangely the Perfesser is one of the more masterful standhunters for whitetails I have ever known. Thereby hangs a tale illustrating the effectiveness of camouflage in the cause of staying unfound. Before I knew him I found a ground blind from which the Perfesser had taken a buck a few days earlier. It was a masterpiece of location, construction and camouflage. The first morning I sat in that stand I got a whitetail buck; that evening my hunting partner was the occupant and took a doe.

A year or two later, the story goes, the Perfesser decided his old stand had gone sour, its cover being blown, so to speak, and commenced building a new one, the veritable chameleon's hideout of deer stands. He located this one high up on the half-burned brush pilings from land clearing, and carefully whittled, sanded and spray painted it until it was nothing but just more burned bush.

The rest of the story comes to me from unusually unreliable sources:

"How'd it work?" one good old boy asks another.

"Nobody knows; he could never find it again."

The absolutely definitive survival pack is essential: not in case of getting lost, but as insurance against getting found. My research proves that many of last fall's found-outs were not properly equipped; thus their friends worried too much about them, called in the helicopters promptly and thereby caused their buddies the acute embarrassment of being found.

There is absolutely nothing wrong with being lost. Some superb hunters argue that the best hunting begins when you are absolutely unconcerned with time and direction. Remember that marvelous scene in William Faulkner's "The Bear," where Ike takes off his watch and compass and hangs them on the bush before entering the wilderness to get serious about hunting the bear? No, lost is an honorable state; what is shameful, embarrassing, is getting found. To prevent this, it is not enough merely to have a day pack full of all manner of goodies: you must advertise, let everyone know it, so, back at camp, when one of your buddies notices it is midnight and you are not back yet, another will say:

"Forget it, he's okay. Could stay out a month and perform heart surgery with all that stuff he's got with him. . . . Why don't you pour me another drop of that great Scotch of his?"

Everyone knows what I carry: knives, first aid kit, chemical fire starter, TV Guide, waterproof matches, lighter, ax, a couple of small pots containing Earl Grey tea bags and dried soup, Eat-More bars, rope and string, flashlight, sheet plastic, two space blankets, you name it. As I do this inventory I notice a survival flare gun someone slipped in there when I was not looking. Out! Out, damned tattletale, for which there is no purpose other than being found. Everyone but my wife is impressed with my survival pack. She believes I am a little old for the solitary hunting I love. For a recent birthday, her gift was a phone installed at the stump ranch so I can check in when I am out of the woods.

What is inevitable, if I have not phoned by 6:00 P.M., is that I will hear the *whop whop* of helicopters by 6:10. I know it, and it ruins my life. There are a couple of answers. The rules do not require me to phone if she knows someone reliable is staying with me. What she does not know is that, to me, "reliable" is a person who is not uptight about getting lost, who has confidence in my survival kit and will not call, particularly if he does not even know the cabin has a removable phone on a wall jack, let alone that I have hidden the set under my bed. But if all precautions fail, the face-saving bottom line of a truly complete survival kit is the one it permits you to toss off when the noise and junk storm of search and rescue descends upon you:

"You guys got nothing better to do than spoil a man's winter camp out?"

But you have to cross-examine carefully if you are to go the decoy companion route. The year after the Perfesser, Joe Holloman, defensive safety of the Edmonton Eskimos and a veteran North Carolina hunter, was my guest at the stump ranch.

"Ever worry about getting lost, Joe?" I asked.

At the time I took great comfort in his impeccable answer: "Shee . . . oot, no, I been lost hundreds of times."

But in these perilous times, where getting found has

reached epidemic proportions, the person who is truly dedicated to avoiding the disease will ask a whole series of additional questions, starting:

"Ever been found out, Joe?"

18

There's No Free Mutt

O NE-MAN DOGS ARE WONDERFUL, BUT BEWARE THE ONE-DOG man. That is what I always try to do when I deliver my weekly column to the newsroom. But this day, as on most, Lennie Delete was on the desk.

"Hey, Bob," he said, "get you into a good dog for free."

"A Labrador, I bet," I sighed.

"Right on! There's a free one offered in today's classifieds."

"Lennie, there's no such thing as a free dog."

"Sure there is, it's right here: Quote. 'Free to a good home. Two-year-old Labrador. I'm a pretty good bird dog.' Unquote."

"Those ads are a code, Lennie. The owner's trying to deal with his guilt about what he's doing to the dog, yet he's put just enough truth in it to prevent being sued by anyone sucker enough to take the mutt."

"Now, you're going to have to explain that, Bob."

"The good home bit always means that the dog does not like the home he has now, runs away a lot and costs a fortune in pound fees. Either that or we're evicting the S.O.B. for constantly humping grandma's knee or swallowing the neighbors' poodles or pit bulling the postman. . . ."

"Awww, you're exaggerating."

"Okay. How about 'moving, must give away'? Surely the

only logical translation is: 'This cur got us evicted once, but never again.'"

"Sounds reasonable."

"Remember that setter of Hoot Squires, everyone's favorite acreage owner?"

"Yah. He told me about it over multi beer one night. Pretty emotional scene. Advised him to see a shrink. But that was no free dog. Hoot claims he paid $300 for it."

"He did so. That's what made it so bad. Old Hoot knows there's no free munch or mutt. He thought paying something would ward off whatever was wrong with it. But I know it started off as a free dog."

"How so?"

"A reader, the owner, phoned. He wanted to know if I knew of a good home for a free two-year-old pointer that likes to hunt, has a friendly disposition, with a pedigree going clear back to old Abe Lincoln's quail-hunting dog."

"Sounds great."

"Sure. So I asked him how come such a deal for sweet tweet?"

"'It's either that or the wife,' he said."

"Women are a dime a dozen, but a good dog is hard to find, I told him."

"'You believe it, I believe it, but my kids . . . no way,' he said. So I thought it was one of your typical jealousy cases. You know, Lennie, one day Doc Moller is sweethearting and honeying that cute Brittany bitch of his, and his old woman observes: 'How come you never sweet-talk me like that?' Doc comes right back: 'You never pointed bird one, nor retrieved any, neither.'"

"Anyhow, I told Hoot and he takes the dog, insists on writing a cheque and for too much to boot. First night, and every night and day since, he discovers 'friendly' means exclusively with other dogs. Never stops talking, that pointer, to every other dog and coyote, too, from his kennel to the correction line and other points beyond the range of human hearing.

"Those code words are funny, if you get to thinking about them. Not so much with hunting dogs, but you often see 'adorable' in the free ads. Translation? Dumb as a sack full of drowned kittens. 'Loves kids,' or 'loyal, courageous family dogs?' Tears the throat out of any adult, including mom and dad."

"What about 'likes to hunt'?" Lennie asks.

"Oh, Hoot's pointer is all hunt. The question is who for? All's you've got is a long dash in orbit out there on the horizon, flushing little dots, apostrophes and quotation marks of pheasants. Meanwhile, back at Mission Control, old Hoot is hollerin' and otherwise popping eyeballs and a hernia to boot, blowing the pea out his umpteenth whistle of the day."

"Maybe," Lennie said, "'free to a good home' also means 'we lack the guts to give the S.O.B. the third eye ourselves.'"

"You know, for an editor, you catch on real quick. . . . Years back my old man got caught short of dogs in high hunting season and took a *free* Springer. Those were the years the show breeders were crossing corn brooms with doormats and turning the breed into basket cases, but this one was billed as 'insatiable hunter.' First time out—I'm fourteen, eh?—I have to talk the Guv out of giving that one the 12-gauge third eye, as he lay on the far bank of a full canal, eating his limiting out pheasant of the day."

"Next day we traded our 'insatiable hunter' for Clancy of Avondale, a.k.a. Buster, both our lifetime's best-ever dog. Old Buster did it all; we figured he even had a larger English vocabulary than your average sports writer. Funny . . . he became a free dog himself in his retirement. He got full of arthritis and would cry when we couldn't take him hunting. So a farmer friend offered him a good home. First crop protection hunt the next September, Buster took off first shot. After the flight was over, they found the old guy, dab in the center of the field, guarding a dog-pile of ducks because he didn't know where his one man was, or who else to take them to. . . ."

"Now there," Lennie said, "was one good free dog."

"Sure, at the end. I admitted that."

"No, I mean right from the start."

"Come on, the old man traded for him."

"Sure! Free mutt for free mutt's still free."

"Hell, Lennie, even you, hungover, are worth ten cents a pound."

"Sometimes I wonder. But okay. Buster's owner didn't think of him as a free dog; thought, in fact, he was getting something for him."

"Right. You have to be careful. There is so a free lunch: every single one ever eaten by a free bird dog."

"By the way," Lennie said, "I suppose old Buster was yet another in your long line of those rocking horse, bobtail Brittanies?

"Well, now you mention it, no. Buster was the first in Dad's and my long line of Labradors."

"Hah! Lennie pounced. "That rests that case! Maybe we should reconsider whether he was free or not. Let me see that ad again. How about we parlay this free Lab into pure gold by working a trade for old Hoot's born-again, paid-in-full pointer?"

19

The Cuzif Conundrum
(A Bluffer's Guide to Gutting)

ON DAY-ONE OF MY THIRD DEER SEASON, THE WORST THING I had been dreading happened: I up and shot at my first deer and he fell stone dead! Suddenly I remembered I was hunting alone.

As a child I kept an imaginary menagerie of playmates, and did all the voices. Now thirty-something, staring dumbfounded at my downed forkhorn mule deer there in that dusky swamp, I summoned my imaginary but faithful hunting buddy.

"Now what do I do?" I wailed.

A huge hand pointed from the heavens to the belly of my buck and Almighty Mouth (who somehow always sounds suspiciously like my late, sainted father) boomed: "Guts're in there, boy, get'm out."

So I tried to remember all the books and articles I had pored over about how you field-dressed a deer, should you ever be so unfortunate as to get one.

The instructions are always clear enough to a point, then lapse into vagueness, then threat: for example, "Be careful. The bladder lies within the pelvis and you don't want to cut or break it."

Saying *be careful* to an excited hunter embarked on thoracic, then urological surgery with a very sharp knife is worse than the common practice of handing a new .22 rifle to a couple of forkedhorny teenage humans, then telling them to be careful. They don't know how. Even the material with pictures and drawings, or so it always seemed to me, had the black censored strip over the private or hard parts.

My old friend, guide and mountain man Thorny Razzleberry learned instant field dressing his apprenticeship year wrangling and gutting for his old man, Horny, when he had to field-dress more that ninety of God's critters in one season, from mighty moose down to puny pronghorn. I once saw him do two deer in three minutes flat. It was too fast to see, so I had to ask Thorny what he did about that vague point, the hard part.

"Oh, that there's just your ordinary eight bone, what I call the *cuzif.*"

"Cuzif?"

"Old Ayrab word. . . . Cuzif it warn't thar, dummy, the innards'd just plop out, slick as spit through a tin horn, and I'd do 'em in one minute per, guaranteed."

"So, how do you handle the cuzif?"

"Well, thar's your corers and your splitters. Sort of deep fillysophickle question for humans that don't matter none to the critter no more cuz he's dead."

So I did both to be sure and philosophically correct with that first buck.

Though I have now done the chore many times since, I have never been satisfied I am doing it the best or even the same way each time. Sometimes the bladder seems absent. At other times it is obvious, taut, plump and pulsating, like an old steam boiler ready to blow.

One time the golden opportunity presented itself to do the definitive, illustrated monograph on standard operating procedures for field dressing ungulates. For the first time I was hunting with Doc Moller, the root canal millionaire, and his friend, Calvin, a medical illustrator.

The Doc promised he would not field dress any deer he got until I was present, so I could observe and photograph his revolutionary surgical procedures. My words and photos and Calvin's drawings, all explicating the inexplicable, would produce a best-seller, maybe even a video, called *Utter Gutter*, or something visceral.

The Doc did get a nice whitetail buck, and with all assembled, he commenced to cut a whole inch-wide section out of the cuzif from the inside with one of those wire survival saws. But he had made only one pull when pungent musk scented the crisp air and the dreaded yellow stain we warn kids about spread over the snow.

"First time I ever saw that," Calvin whispered. Me too. I folded up my tripod.

Doc Moller lost his nerve as totally as one of his root canals, quit hunting and took up catch-and-release fly-fishing, then fled to exile on the west coast where he works as an Orca oral hygienist for a marine museum.

After Thorny Razzleberry had become the great outdoors writer who "covers the outdoors west like a July blizzard," he claimed to have developed a surefire, axless method of splitting the cuzif, inspired by having seen someone disjoint ruffed grouse by standing on the wings and pulling up on the legs.

"This we gotta see," my old friend Griz announced, so we invited Thorny along with our usual bunch to push a little bush.

As usual, somebody just had to ruin a good hunt by getting a deer. After the front stuff, including paunch, was rolled out on the ground, we all gathered around to watch Thorny perform. He planted one foot on each of the buck's spread hind legs, squatted like a Bulgarian weight lifter, grabbed the tail in both hands and strained upward, eyes bulging.

There was a crack, a thump, then a grunt as the tail gave way and fluttered to the ground like a feather from a shot pheasant. The pheas . . . er . . . Thorny tumbled and spun, flippity flop, against the fall sky, then splattered into the gut pile like a grasshopper onto a windshield.

When Thorny temporarily regained consciousness, the first thing he heard was Griz getting to the punch line of the old joke about the hunters who rushed their wounded buddy to the hospital. Eventually a weary surgeon told them he might have saved their buddy if only they had not field dressed him.

Next time Thorny came to, the boys were arguing whether his dive deserved 9.6s across the board or whether his tuck was not tight enough and his entry into the paunch a dab splashy.

"Hell," Griz said, "he deserves straight tens for artistic impression for all this great organic camo he splattered all over us."

Many hunters have a designated gutter no farther than a faint whimper away. I have unwittingly played the role a time or three myself.

One evening I was wandering a series of finger draws, trying to chouse deer up into a big field on top where Fifty-Fifty Fred, our beloved judge, was on stand. When two shots sounded I just carried on chousing for an hour and a half or so. After all, a game plan is a game plan. Besides, it would insult the skills of the Judge to arrive, panting, on the scene before the echo of his shot dies away, for gosh sake.

But sometimes nothing works. In the dark I found Hizzoner by homing in on his muttering. There he was, *corpus delicti* uncut and untagged, flipping his way through his license booklet, chanting it to himself, over and over, like a mantra. I have to assume that the poor man had been disabled by a virulent form of retroactive buck fever because I am not at liberty to assume an officer of the court would ever procrastinate.

By feel and flashlight I was able to convince the Judge that it was a whitetail button buck and sort out his tags for him. Then I cored and split in dark so pitch a man could not find his own cuzif with a dowsing rod. The Judge babbled on about how he hit that buck, running, right behind the ear, but could not imagine how a great rifleman like him ever missed that first shot . . . unless . . . could that buck have been standing too still?

To this day, Fifty-Fifty Fred can recite, verbatim, from memory, the entire Alberta Wildlife Certificate, including Environment Canada's Sunrise–Sunset timetable on the back for eleven areas of the province, week by week, for three months. But he now carries a vest pocket New Testament with him to preach the last rites next time he is awaiting deliverance by arrival of the designated gutter.

My chance to pass on all I have learned about field dressing came half a dozen years ago as I was on my way to a lawyering house call in good deer country. I went via a legendary back road to see how the season was going.

I bailed out beside a car in the borrow pit, behind which the young fellow who had flagged me down was contemplating a buck he had dragged a long way, judging by the marks in the snow.

"Uh . . . better hand me a dollar, quick," I said, after one look at his mule deer buck.

"Why?"

"Legal advice . . . retainer . . . seal my lips . . . solicitor–client privilege. That buck's illegal and they patrol this road heavily."

He argued briefly that the tiny brow tines should count to turn the forkhorn into a legal three-point. The regulations out of my rig settled that one.

"You better get that buck done and loaded quick. Better still, load him first and do him elsewhere."

"But . . .

"Should turn you in, but you wouldn't have drug him out to the road if you thought you were doing anything wrong."

"I was looking for help, and I get a mouthpiece in a suit and tie. What do I do next?"

"I'm never dressed for aiding and abetting an illegal gutting," I said. "Guts're in there, get 'em out. Almighty Mouth may be a ventriloquist, but that does not make me his dummy."

"What?"

"Nothing."

"But what do I do about . . . down . . . there?"

"Oh . . . that's just your common cuzif. Core it or split it, but beware of the bladder. . . ."

20

How to Get Permission

I F PERMISSION TO HUNT AND FISH HAD BEEN EASY AND SIMPLE
to get, it would not have been necessary to invent poaching.

Whoa! I can hear the howls of outrage already at the jux-
taposition of the mere concept of *trespassing* with that loaded
word *poaching*. "Everybody does it," (trespasses) as our teenagers
always plead about anything, but we all know, deep down, that
poachers are always somebody else. I have known life-long
poachers whose delicate feelings were so hurt when they finally
got caught that they ended their careers—quit hunting and
fishing—then and there, almost as though they'd show the rest
of us just what they thought of us.

Sorry if anyone is insulted, but American and British dic-
tionaries are unanimous on the point: poaching is to "hunt or
catch game or fish illegally, especially by trespassing on private
property." Trespassing is simply being on private property
without permission, for any reason, notwithstanding those
most oxymoronic of all signs: No Trespassing Without
Permission.

North Americans like asking permission about as much as
they like being very selective about which other fish and game
laws they personally choose to obey. Thus, because there are so
many, it is simple to find poachers in North America, most of

whom will reveal their methods at great length to a trustworthy journalist they know will protect his source and respect their confidence with a nonattribution agreement. Thus, one of my old friends, who wishes to remain anonymous, Percy Guttman, says about the whole subject: "It ain't so much the gettin' in as the getaway that's tricky." Now, that's an expert opinion. Percy's present address is c/o Easy Time Correctional Institute. Something about having miscounted and mismatched tags and deer one moonless night last September.

The absolute master I have ever known at getting permission was also the best pheasant road hunter I have ever known. He came from California for two weeks or a month or more to my old hometown every fall for nearly forty consecutive pheasant seasons. Call him Cal. When my Dad could not get away, I got to guide. When you rode with Cal you soon learned that one superb eye was looking out for roadside pheasants, while the other was on constant alert for the absolute worst signs: No Hunting: I Don't Mean Maybe; Trespassers Will Be Shot—Survivors Will Be Prosecuted. Cal would have loved the one I saw down in our old neck of the woods last fall: No Trespassing: Beware Rattlesnakes. The last rattlesnake seen there was the serpent that caused such misery to Adam, Eve and the rest of their extended family—all of us.

Cal had been hearing about a superb patch of cover, but nobody, absolutely nobody, could get around the hard-drinking Hungarian who owned it. The vicinity of that cover drew Cal's mettle like a magnet. Early one hunting day we were both eyeing a super piece of cover, then we spotted a sign saying, as best as I recall: Hunters No Good For Sh——! It might even have said something offensive.

Cal wheeled right into the farmyard and bailed out. "Bring the jug, boy," he said. Years later I remember the huge fridge stuffed full of beer upstairs in the kitchen and the dumpling of a wife who had to trudge up and down to the ancient ice-box in the basement for frivolities like butter or, worse, milk. The lord and master wore a battered felt fedora at the break-fast table and smoked an old, black curved pipe that smelled like an outhouse fire. He grew a lush handlebar mustache and had a slow, hooded look to his eyes, like a sleepy rattlesnake. But he took the jug, straight up, when offered. Before he could take a pull, Dumpling plunked two jelly jars down on the table. "No, no, use glass," she said.

"I'm boss," he roared, and drank so deeply from the bottle that it sounded like a flushing toilet.

Eventually the kid was dismissed with full permission to some of the finest pheasant cover I and all my dogs have yet to see to this day.

"I'll call when I need to be picked up," Cal, my mentor, said. As I remember it, the call was several days coming.

Before he returned to California when each season was over, Cal always threw a massive party. It was wedding dance rules: the whole town and countryside were invited. Sometimes it went on for three days. The man was a legend. Eventually he, and we, would have permission from the head rattlesnake in the Garden of Eden if we wanted.

Well, that's one way, a very old way to get permission. But these days the method would be regarded as at least an unhealthy lifestyle, if not certain death. By rights, Cal should have had a liver as gray, jagged, hard and holey as a chunk of lava rock. Not so. His was as pink and soft as a Nerf ball. Cal died peace-fully in his bed in his midseventies the night after he had poached his last pheasant on my farm. He'd gotten permission once from my deceased father and naturally assumed it was forever, no matter who became the owner.

Cal was a positive inspiration to a young lout. Some of my best secret spots that stay that way have resulted from my tackling the toughest owners of the most obnoxious No TRESPASSING, NO HUNTING, NO FISHING, NO NOTHING signs. A varmint hunting fanatic I know specializes in antihunting females who are also grieving former owners of poodles and pussy cats. He firmly believes that as long as people will persist in keeping such creatures, coyotes, bobcats and that ilk will never become endangered let alone extinct. When he hears of someone who has lost a string of pets to those awful coyotes, he goes around, shows the lady his cherished decoy, a full-body mount of a mangy, rat-tailed coyote, and gets grateful, tearful permission to call and execute every last one of her sleek, fat, prebaited varmints. In the field he frequently employs full-body mounts of a toy poodle and a Siamese cat in conjunction with this custom yap-and-purr call. In season he also gets permission to hunt deer on the property simply by being careful to whine regularly to the lady about how taking care of her problem has consumed all his preseason deer scouting time.

Similar is the archery gambit employed on owners of prime deer habitat who are not necessarily antihunting so much as worried about firearms. There are gents I know who could not draw a bow with either a come-along or an HB pencil who have tree forts up all during archery season, impressing the landowner with their dedication to duty and making sure he hears every hard-luck story of the deer too distant for a bow. Somehow they always wind up as the only firearm hunters on earth with permission, up those same trees, bright and early opening day of rifle season.

This sympathy factor is critical for many who do get permission. I have known a master from back in the days when he would turn up with his two sons and mention to the landowner that he would like to start the kids out right, getting permission, then hunting on a truly prime piece of habitat. A couple of falls ago, one of those same kids, now middle-aged, was getting permission by explaining how his old Dad was out there in the rig and how he'd like the old gent to have one last truly fine hunt, right here and now, on earth.

The old gent himself usually preferred to get permission from the woman of the house whenever possible. He regularly practiced and cultivated the folksy touch. He would carefully look around as he walked to the door for something, anything he could admire, comment on and chat about.

"My, my," he would gush, "you grow them flowers yourself? I ain't seen hollyhocks like that since my dear old Mom commenced pushin' up daisies."

Once we drove up a farm driveway that was bordered with glass jugs of cheap purple gasoline in various stages of being bleached white preliminary to dyeing with margarine dye into expensive orange gas. He pointed out to that lady that some of them fine jugs were possibly valuable antiques, and she should check it out. I am not making this up.

Plain audacity, verve and nerve can frequently turn the trick. Asking the landowner out hunting or fishing with you— on his own property—sometimes works. What often turns the trick is if you happen to own the world's best bird dog or are known to be a world-class moose- or elk-caller, a master at nymph-fishing without bobber, something, anything you can show the owner, preferably in and on his own fine cover, or along his stretch of river.

Sometimes you have to ease into it with a form of the game veteran hunters and fishers often play with each other: "You show me yours, I'll show you mine." Take the landowner hunting or fishing on one or two of your own less-favored places. If things work perfectly and the hunting or fishing is lousy and you are royally skunked, then you can do the pitch. Surely any hunter or fisher knows how to blather on about how that's always the way when you want to show somebody something really good and how you are plumb out of ideas about where to take him next, and is there any place he'd like you and him to try?

These are only some of the lengths the very few people who bother to ask at all will go to get permission. Most North Americans just will not bother. Those latter types, the vast majority, should consider what happens and what you do when you are found without.

Another old veteran gave me a pungent line on the most solemn oath of mine that I would not quote him. Thorny Razzleberry, of Site #1, RR#1, East Anguish, Alberta (just turn left at the antler stack, then drive on toward the cloud of crows), said, and I quote: "Rule number one for the poacher is that it is easier to beg forgiveness than to ask permission."

Outright
Lies

21

How to Beg Forgiveness

So there you are, blissfully huntin' or fishin' and a faint, far-off sound causes you to look up. Out there on the horizon whirls a dust devil that shouts faintly. As it gets closer it is a whirlwind that yells. Soon you are in the direct path of a cyclone building to a tornado that roars profanely of persecution, prosecution, yea, even death.

Gradually it dawns on you that you are about to find out if it is truly easier to beg forgiveness than ask permission.

At times like this a trespassing old English professor of my acquaintance says his only comfort is a wise quote from *The Water Babies:* "a keeper is only a poacher turned outside in, and a poacher a keeper turned inside out." In other words, they are kindred souls: landowners themselves are some of the worst poacher–trespassers and have not only heard them all, but may themselves have at least used, if not invented, some of the best excuses. Thus, you may expect some sympathy there, but be careful. Yes, trespassers are invariably "keepers," either neighbors from the vicinity or "landowners" from the city who would forthwith call the cops if you turned your kids loose in their backyards, kindled a fire and settled down with a beer and the missus for a weekend weenie bake.

That "babies" reminds me that many veteran trespassers

say it really helps to have a kid or three along. They at least temper the gale-force language and violence of the cyclone and might even evoke some sympathy. Why do you think these "take a kid fishing/hunting" programs are so popular, besides the training of future trespasser—poachers, that is? Some truly progressive sporting goods stores are now advertising kids for rent.

Here's how it can work. A couple of seasons ago I watched a rig screech to a halt on a paved road. One big and one small boy bailed out, rested rifles on the hood and blazed away over blaze-orange No TRESPASSING—No HUNTING signs at a little forkhorn mule deer browsing peacefully in an alfalfa field that was also occupied by a herd of beloved and valuable Morgan horses.

So I took the license number and told the big one I was going to see the owner of the land and he could follow if he dared or cared. The big boy, obviously the father, immediately commenced to snivel:

"Aw guys," then he indicated his forkedhorny fellow human, "this is his first time hunting, and I wanted it to be a memorable day." No, we did not puke, but did leave the matter of charges up to the landowner. Me and my companion went immediately to check for wounded horses—or deer. Days later the landowner thanked me, but said he was not pressing charges: "I accepted his apology, but not his explanation."

If you are too cheap or smart to own or even rent kids, what else can you do to beg forgiveness? Consider the frequently-employed hot-pursuit gambit, which requires a much smaller investment than kids, either owned or rented.

Obtain and carry the most powerful water pistol money can buy, quick, before they too become prohibited weapons or you have to hold a Firearms Acquisition Certificate before you can buy one. Load it with theatrical blood. Carry it with you where you can get at it quickly while hunting. Quick-draw immediately when you hear or see that dust devil and promptly squirt down a blood trail ahead and behind. When the tornado blows in, admit you know you are trespassing, but insist that no ethical person—let alone hunter—would allow a wounded animal to suffer, even though most Game and Wildlife Acts do not permit entering private land without permission for the purpose of recovering wounded game.

Should your irate landowner check out either end of the trail and a long way beyond the range of your pistol, you can always chuckle as how you never could be sure which way an animal was going just from blood sign, and anyhow:

"Ain't that always the way for the blood sign to peter out like that. Guess he ain't hurt too bad, but do you mind if I keep on lookin'?" (This is important if what you were really seeing was cover so good that it might enable you to turn up in the landowner's yard later to show him that "wounded critter" finally got put out of his misery.)

The clear implication, indeed the prerequisite of all this, of course, is that you "wounded" the animal on land on which you had permission, and many of even the most irate trespass tornadoes will not charge you. As a matter of fact, this one worked on me last season. I found the guy's quad on my land loaded with a head-shot antlerless mule deer. He was elsewhere, maybe laying down a good back trail out of the land next door for the dead critter, which, when I found the hunter, I suggested he come back and tag.

The most general gambit with many variations is the lost or straying sheep syndrome:

"You don't mean to stand there and tell me this ain't (name the only landowner you know in the vicinity's) place?"

This is especially good if you are merely scouting to see if a place is prime for serious trespass, being good country and unoccupied. One day this past spring a rig roared down a winding forest driveway into the yard of an occupied cabin, then reversed into a bootlegger turn that dropped one wheel through the grill and into the fire pit. Down another mile-and-a-half-long driveway, another bootlegger did $500 to $1,000 damage to the landowner's parked rig, bounced off into the muskeg and got stuck. Unfortunately the seized rig was not worth half the damages. In the first case the young lady said, "Sorry about that," but the lout with her muttered darkly about whiplash and unmarked excavations. In the second case the landowner caught hell for leaving so little room for a man to turn around. First case said a neighbor told her the driveway was a good route to the crik; second claimed he had merely missed the turn onto the main road as he came out from visiting one of the neighbors.

A further refinement of this gambit is to claim that someone actually gave you permission to hunt this very land, and get very aggressive about it. One opening morning of pheasant season several years ago, a couple of gents tried to throw me off my own farm, claiming a neighbor had given them permission to hunt there. They demanded, in fact, that I prove I owned the place.

To their intense disgust I had the county landowner map in the rig and the bad manners to ask them to show me the precise location of the neighbor they alleged gave them permission. Seems the map was a little out of date for that sort of thing. "Must've been printed before they moved in." In fact the landowner's name seemed to have slipped their collective mind, but they did offer to take me there, correctly gambling that I and my companions, human and canine, would prefer to get the season under way chasing pheasants rather than tracking down weak alibis.

These guys were masters who actually made me feel so

guilty for owning the land that I invited them to come back in the evening when the hunting was usually very good and when the owner and friends would be elsewhere.

Actually I do have some sympathy for stories of this kind because it is an astonishing fact that neighbors will often give somebody permission to hunt or fish your land. Generally these are neighbors who themselves routinely trespass on your land to hunt, fish, pick berries, mushrooms, etcetera, they having bulldozed and burned all the habitat on their own land. Because you fear their tendencies to slash and burn, you say nothing, and they translate this to all and sundry as "Aw . . . good old Joe don't mind; he hunts and fishes himself."

For years a couple of genial farming gents gave me permission to hunt the world's greatest weed-choked ditch for pheasants. Suddenly I discovered it was not their ditch when confronted one day by a very large and irate Lithuanian who I knew had a black belt in the Oriental martial art of mayhem. The deal we made was that if he would not cross the ditch to "clean my clock," as he threatened, I would not have to unload my shotgun as a safety precaution, and I would never darken his ditch again.

That county landowner map is often touted as an aid to getting permission for people who care about details like that. More importantly it can also be a useful adjunct to the story that you have wandered off course from land on which you had—honest!—permission. Judicious customizing can color green, for public land, all sorts of land that really is not. In my favorite hunting and fishing area this will be credible because everyone knows the latest version of the map is a joke, with the Municipal District having colored "private" hundreds of sections and quarter sections that really are public land.

If you claim you had permission on the land next door, that better be true, because it is likely your alibi will be checked. That "public" land you were hunting better not be a national or provincial park unless you want to occupy public property in the immediate future, doing big time, complete with guards and bars.

One suggestion: never, ever, after having taken your tongue-lashing, brightly respond, "Well, now can I have permission?" As a member of the Alberta bar, I am advising you that, in virtually any North American jurisdiction, that is a clear admission you knew permission should have been requested in the first place and wasn't. Asking after the fact, or act, is guaranteed to pump back at least to cyclone intensity a tornado that had blown himself down to a mere dust devil and inspire him to pollute any nearby watercourse with the worthless remains of a person like yourself.

But some outdoors people are just never properly prepared and equipped for the rigors of their outdoors pursuits. What do you do if you have no kids along, no water pistol, no landowner map, not even uncustomized? As a last resort you could fall to your knees and fall back on something your sainted old Mom drove you to as a kid—Sunday school—and the fact this is a Christian country, after all, and that may even be a Christian tornado blowing in. Timing is everything with this one. Make sure you are at the right part just as he has left his rig and stomped up to you, and speak up in a fervent voice, like Miss Devout taught you to do so long ago, praying:

". . . forgive us our trespasses as we forgive those who trespass against us. . . ."

22

Truth in Angling

NOT OFTEN WOULD A PRAIRIE LAD EVEN READ, LET ALONE BE frozen with fear, by an outdoors magazine article on salt-water angling. But I read everything I find on the subject, as it is my mania within a hobby: I fish the salt every rare chance I get.

This article concerned problems encountered by the large fishing tournaments in Florida. Increasingly the public has expressed outrage over the display of rare and endangered species piled on docks and hung on scales at weigh-in time. In response many of the tournaments have gone the catch-and-release route. Human nature and the common perception of anglers have caused another set of problems related to one question: how can you be sure the contestant caught the fish of such and such a species and of such and such a size when and where he swears up and down he did?

What chilled me solid is that the article reported that some of the big tournaments have taken to employing the polygraph, more commonly called the lie detector. There, I feared, went my cherished dream and all my careful groundwork laid for catching the new Alberta record brown or rainbow trout.

Many times in recent years I have fished in the first honor system fishing tournament I ever heard of, the club derby of the Calgary Hook and Hackle Club on the lower Bow River, where, the whole world now knows, there are monstrous brown and rainbow trout. One day, I know, I will be able to attend the closing ceremonies and advise the committee that I have not only caught the derby winner, but the new Alberta record. In fact, I have inscribed the dimensions of the existing provincial record browns and rainbows inside my hatband to remind me.

Other preparations must be made for such an event. The first year, in the presence of witnesses, a fish took all my fly line and backing in one minute flat as it surged for the nearest ocean at least a thousand miles away. Recently there have been reliable reports of fish taken in the thirty-two to thirty-three-inch-long category. Or could that just be other anglers preparing their "groundwork?" No matter, in one of the derbies I lost another trout that a reliable and sober witness swore was thirty-two inches between the eyes.

In the earlier derbies you were vulnerable to an attack founded on the legal maxim that there is no murder if you cannot produce the *corpus delicti*. But since the government of Alberta forbade the murder of large trout on the lower Bow, the world will just have to accept that a person really would release a record-breaking brown or rainbow trout, simply because he has to.

But that polygraph idea bothered me. Back in the days when I was doing a lot of criminal law, I observed some of the smoothest liars I ever knew break out in cold sweats, trembling and hyperventilating, or in uncontrollable laughter at the mere Crown offer of a lie detector test. It turns out it is appropriate to mention these physiological responses.Here is what the 24th edition of *Dorland's Illustrated Medical Dictionary* has to say about the polygraph:

> *An instrument for simultaneously recording several mechanical or electrical impulses, such as respiratory movements, pulse wave, blood pres-*

sure, and the psychogalvanic reflex. Such phenomena reveal emotional reactions which are of use in detecting deception.

"Of use in detecting deception"—not conclusive, in other words, and that was the wise counsel back in my criminal law days. Plainly it was felt that the polygraph was not totally reliable: truth-tellers could fail, passers could be liars. When applied to anglers, I had only to think of some of my buddies to predict a whole batch of problems for the polygraph. My friend Griz suffers from hypertension and is into meditation or self-hypnosis, by which he can control his pulse rate and lower his raging blood pressure by many points. In fact, his doctor has noted the mere start of fishing season lowers Griz's blood pressure below that of a hibernating bear. Then there is Gutley, who is in such fantastic physical condition that he can bring ten simultaneous whoppers to a credible conclusion without drawing a breath. Psychogalvanic reflex? Let me offer you Neversweat Nugent, whose skin, owing to a rare medical condition, is never sufficiently moist to conduct enough current to short the dynamo in a firefly's ar . . . uh . . . behind.

It may be, in fact, that all these gents possess many of the physiological peculiarities of each of them, as each of them is totally credible. Butter wouldn't melt in the mouths of the pack of them. In other words, if they are liars, they are totally undetectable. Bear in mind that they have developed their skills by playing to the world's toughest audience. New York plays are first tried out in Boston; fishermen first test their whoppers on brother anglers, each of whom has been equipped from birth with a built-in B.S. detector, or has developed an immunity to the stuff through exposure to his own.

Strangely it is not the general public but anglers themselves who have fostered the popular conception that all fishermen are liars. Rest assured that the general public did not demand the polygraph tests in those saltwater tournaments. The public merely wanted an end to the killing of endangered species. It was the anglers who did not trust each other and sought protection from someone doing to them what they would like to do first—if only they had the gall.

Stories without end will attest to the legendary skepticism with which fishermen view other fishermen. Once when I was fishing in Newfoundland, my party came upon an old gent with one shy of a limit of salmon slung from his belt who was fishing for the last one using a peculiar hand motion.

"Some people say I jigs 'em," he explained, "but I'se got the palsy."

Our young guide was scornful: "He's no Newfundlander; he'd lie when 'twasn't even to his advantage."

Another time a fisherman of my acquaintance was going on about an angling writer we both know and contending the writer is an habitual liar in general and in particular on the one occasion we were discussing.

"How do you know he was lying?" I asked.

"His lips were moving."

But of particular relevance to the whole question of fishing tournaments, honor and the skepticism of fishermen is the old story of the immediate, instinctive, unrehearsed response of an angler who was shown the fresh *corpus* of a monstrous fish just caught by a colleague:

"Whoever caught that fish is a liar!"

Thus it is not surprising that the collective response of participants in an honor system fishing tournament should be: "Whoever *says* he caught that fish is a liar!" Add to this the fact that nobody is more frustrated than the anglers themselves at their inability to detect even their own lies and that fishermen are the technology–gadget junkies of the outdoors world, and it is completely logical that they should fasten upon the sonar of the psyche—the polygraph—as the solution to their credibility problem.

Measuring multiphysiological responses aside, each angler knows that every other angler believes his own stories and wants the world to believe them, too. Without objective, hard evidence, it is absolutely impossible for another angler, let alone a mere polygraph, to prove a person a liar who is absolutely convinced that what he is saying is God's own truth. Face it: in their hearts these people do not want to catch liars; they want the fish the liars say they caught to be the truth. After all, the next whopper caught—or told—may be your own.

It came as no surprise but as considerable comfort to read later in the magazine article that started all this that so far the lie detector has not rejected the story of any tournament winner. The public should be prepared for another story, very soon, that a winner verified by the polygraph has been proven by independent, objective, hard evidence to have been a liar when he said he caught a fish of a certain species and yea dimensions in such and such a location, employing the prescribed methods. Anyone who knows anglers will know that "liar" will be able to pass another polygraph when he says that the photographs, the private detectives and the eyewitnesses are mistaken at best and a pack of liars at worst.

Generally I have opposed the burgeoning of technology in angling as detracting from the experience and probably being unsporting and unfair to the quarry. But the introduction of the polygraph to tournament angling has good implications for the sport and the resource that were probably not envisaged by the pioneers of the innovation: the miracle of converting a fisherman's lie into God's own truth. A new sport—fishing in the mind—may be the next logical development. Certainly a lot of trophy fish could be taken without killing anything, without even fishing for them, for that matter. Think about it.

As for myself, I believe I will amend those statistics inside my hat band. The lower Bow is a great river: there is no reason at all why a man should not shoot for world records. Now what are the dates for the Hook and Hackle Derby? Come to think of it, who cares about dates?

23

I and the Egg
(Caviar Emptor, Ernie)

THE STYX IN SPATE: SMELTED FROM A BLIZZARD IN THE foothills above hell, the river surged around and out of Hades, bending always to the left, no matter how far upstream you fished; yellow waters bounding and rebounding from huge boulders, bursting into sulfurous spray. On the left, the bank of the dead was dark beneath rolling and grinding thunderheads; on the right, the bank of the living was warm green and gold, bathed in soft, diffuse sunlight. Here the Styx runs generally north and south, over boulders, bones, wrecks and rubble.

Ideal stone fly habitat, I thought, hopefully.

In the shallows, giant black creatures, like tiny, spoiled lobsters, crawled onto the rocks and bushes. The chitin would split over the wing cases of the nymph, then a winged creature—like a miniature *Pterodactyl*—would crawl out.

Yuk! Bugs! I thought, revoltingly.

High above the trees, on the bank of the living, and against the shafts of light, clouds of the creatures could be seen flying, drawn always lower and lower toward the water as their bodily burdens burgeoned.

Years ago, on Colorado's Gunnison, I fished my first salmon fly hatches, gradually learning the sweet torture of

148

fishing huge, weighted nymph imitations during the emergence, then savoring the delicious agony of waiting for the wild dry-fly fishing during the "brush" hatch, occurring whenever the winged adults managed to find one another, mate and finally get around to laying their eggs.

Bonanza! I thought, wildly. Salmon flies. Emergence and brush hatch on the same day!

In the warm sunshine over the bank of the living, egg laying was standard, but limited to females only, helicoptering over the flow to jettison their ova. Their fertile eggs are extruded into a claret-colored cluster, which is dropped from heights of three to eight feet above the flow. So dense is the cluster, near the 207.21 atomic weight of lead, that an egg-laying female will lurch upward as though she hit a thermal when the eggs drop. Once the egg mass hits the water, it sinks like lead, then a powerful, water-activated glue adheres it firmly to the bottom.

The best dry-fly fishing to *Pteronarcys* adults takes place when the humidity is high, or when it is actually raining and the egg mass adheres to the female. Then she must descend flush to the surface, dip her ovipositor into the water and fly upstream, permitting the surface tension to pull the egg mass loose, much as a mongrel drags its sphincter over the grass to rid itself of tapeworm. The wake resulting, the fluttering of those capsules of pure protein, drives the trout wild. Everywhere there will be flushes, gushes and gouts of spray as the fish gorge. Every time I experience it, I recall telling myself: *Look at those hawgs!*

Mist had now condensed to rain over the bank of the dead. Females could be seen down on the water, writhing and fluttering, bumping and grinding in the annual rite of regeneration. But not a trout took notice. Then I switched from the dry fly to the weighted nymph until I inflamed my bursitis.

Somewhere I read "most fishermen assume that the fishing is simple during the salmon fly hatch, and sometimes it is remarkably simple when conditions are right. But sometimes it becomes a frustrating puzzle."

Ain't that the truth? I agreed with whoever it was wrote that.

Perhaps these fish changed habits under the influence of those superbly skilled fishermen, the kind who prefer chilled white wines "of the country." But the heresy of these Styx fish drove me around the bend to spy on Charon.

There he was, the dean *emeritus,* the keeper of the Styx, rod hooped, reel whining, in *extremis.*

"What are they taking?" I screamed.

"Speak Italica *like you used to,"* Charon glared.

"Oh," I screamed, *"what are those hawgs taking?"*

"Caviar."

"Beluga?"

"No, salmon," he giggled, saltily.

"Boy! They sure do want salmon eggs!"

"Not salmon eggs, Schwiebert, salmon fly eggs."

"Gee whiz, those hawgs sure do go for salmon fly eggs," I admired.

Several years ago, Charon was becalmed on the bank of his beloved Styx, staring glumly at waters that stared blankly back, unpunctuated by a rise, while a billion salmon flies filled the air with their ritual of recreation. Some deceased angling legend was beside him (he believes it was Arnold Gingrich), flipping the confection called Pearled Peanuts into the air and catching them in his mouth. The candy, with its knobby red surface, and the action, so resembling the salmon fly clusters that were even then splattering like hailstones on the surface of the Styx, were Proust's Madelaine to Charon. Two further years spent with snorkel and scuba gear solved the mystery.

Once he confirmed that these fish were selectively eating the eggs and rejecting the parents, that left only the problem of imitation. How would one reproduce the appropriate mass, silhouette and clumplike shape of the naturals together with their incredible specific gravity?

Lead shot, size BB was the approximate size, and it was discovered that if the BB was recovered from the load of a shotgun shell fired into a sandbox, it would have the appropriate pitted and knobbed clumpishness.

Born of that development, it was a simple matter to partially split the shot and attach it jig-style behind the eye of a size 6 Mustad #3906 hook. All questions of color were resolved by a quick dip in Dracula #13 nail polish.

These simple, clean imitations worked so well that only some perverted, unknown angler of low cunning (and I would like to believe it was me) could have devised the "tassel" on the Sofa Pillow. This is simply the lead-head egg fly attached by six inches of eight-pound nylon behind and to any of the standard dry salmon fly imitations.

This combination is devastating on those drizzly gray days when the adults, females only, must descend right onto the water to be relieved of their burdens. The tassel so completely solves the vexing puzzle of short strikes that some anglers call it the Ha-Ha.

But Charon handed me a half dozen of the basic BBs and directed me to the gray and forbidding bank of the dead.

"*Dead drift,*" *he frowned.*

"*No jiggy jig?*" *I teased.*

"*These eggs stay laid,*" *he muttered, enigmatically.*

"*Dead right,*" *I laughed.*

The perfect tuck cast went out behind a boulder where, Charon had cautioned me, lived a huge, battle-worn old brown trout, transplanted to Hades from Pennsylvania's Le Tort Spring Run. The drift of the nymph stopped, I struck and it stuck.

Snagged, I thought, pointedly.

But the snag moved, gathering speed. Water sheared from the thrumming line like a pane of glass. The reel screamed as the fish made a kamikaze dive dead on for the bank of the living. I had not bothered to change from my two-pound leader and was powerless to turn the fish or stop its run, which went on and on, long after the fish should have crashed into the bank.

Curious, I thought.

I reeled over, wading as I went, until I could see the fluorescent orange line emerging from an underwater cave in the bank.

"Hell!" I screamed, profanely. *"He's gone up a muskrat hole!"*

But life could be felt at the end of the line, so I let everything go limp, sat down on the bank and drew the cork on a bottle of Chablis, Premier Cru, 1983.

"If you catch him, kill him," Charon had said, damningly, *"even for hell, he's over the hill."*

Four hours later, when the brute swam out of the hole, I dropped onto his back. The old warrior surged powerfully, nearly bucking me off, but I got a hand in his gills and lifted, intending, despite Charon, to grant freedom and a dignified, natural death to the fish. What I accomplished, I should have realized sooner, was the "unhorsing" of myself and a soaking to the button of my deerstalker. But I maintained the hold. Then the monster surged, bowed himself caudal to neb and clapped me aside the earhole with a tail like a canoe paddle. Saturn, Neptune and Jupiter spun out of orbit. Somehow, dazed, I found the right pocket to my vest, secured my priest knife and administered the last rites. Over and over.

This was my largest brown trout, a cock fish of twenty-three pounds, with a kype like a sythe and spots like Kruggerands.

Then it was time for a shore lunch. Charon sent me off to

I and the Egg (Caviar emptor, Ernie)

the bushes to gather female salmon flies to collect the appetizer: a saucer of their caviar. Charon flipped a tiny egg mass in the air, caught it in his mouth and raised his glass of a revolutionary little Chilean Chardonnay, 1978, to toast my big brown, now sizzling in the skillet.

"*Praise we now,*" he gulped, "*the lowly egg.*"

24

Surviving the Wild Auction

Blah diddy blah,
Dippity dope,
Woddam I bid
For the pig in a poke?
—AUCTIONEER'S "SONG"

A s I WAS GOING DOWN FOR THE THIRD TIME RECENTLY DURING
a good cry with my banker, the bad rock video of my
immediate past flickered before my eyes. Five wildlife dinner-
auctions in six months—two Trouts Unlimited, one Ducks,
one Pheasants Forever and one Rocky Mountain Elks—had
turned me into a bankruptcy going nowhere to happen.

It is guilt that gets you, slathered on by the good old boy,
steely-eyed, retired business barkers for these organizations
who will accept no excuse. Their specialty is selling tickets to
and getting donations from guilt-ridden doctors, dentists and
accountants who love to hunt and fish, but lack time to work
for conservation. The barkers lure them to the dinner, where
the auctioneer can finish them off. They regard me as a challenge.

"You've done well," one told me recently, "despite all that
downtime working for the cause. So you know better than any-

one that, wildlife-wise, there's too many taking out and not enough putting in."

"But I haven't taken waterfowl one in the past ten years."

"Bob, you had ate more than your lifetime share by the time you was legal age to hunt."

How do those guys know these things? So I bought two tickets, plus made a donation. Instead of prudently abandoning both tickets in some innocent's mailbox, my habit drove me to the dinner. But I did some things right. Despite the modern, blatant, sexist urgings of these affairs to "bring the ladies," I left Herself home and took my survival kit instead: a light lunch and a 10x photographer's magnifying glass. En route I reviewed my survival rules. The ones I followed were: never donate a trip, never buy one, neither, and never bid against a gaunt man with organic fertilizer on his boots and a glint in his eye.

A verbatim report of a recent conversation I had with Counselor Fee Q.C. (Quite Costly), lawyer, out there in Fort Kindling, will illustrate some of what I have been saying:

"Bob, they kept the bar open for two hours, then they started the auction. Dinner was held hostage until after the auction. The excuse was they had to use a different format than Dee You did two weeks earlier."

"Great! The first rule of these things is never close the bar. Now they add: never serve dinner, either. Ducks, hell, they'll be greenheads over greenwings with envy that they didn't think of it first."

"It worked, Bob. First thing I heard when I came to was Bleep Blather, the auctioneer, hollering 'sold to Couns. Fee for $2,000.'"

"Congratulations, what did you buy?"

"Not me, it was the Old Woman waving my hand in a bidding war with Glint Junior Silverspoon over a limited edition spotting scope, just your ordinary Brushwhacker crated up with box, medallion and number. Said she always wanted one to watch the sparrows and magpies at our feeder mug and mutilate each other."

"Glint Junior—the one who inherited the custom feedlot cleaning empire?"

"One and the same, plus now he's into diversification, only he calls it recycling. Whatever, he's your born-again manure millionaire."

"So he's got doo on his boots and dough in the bank?"

"Bob, when Glint Junior writes a cheque, the bank bounces."

"Doesn't write many, though?"

"Guess not. Believes in all the causes. Stink bids a lot. Collects an artist or two. If anyone is going to get a bargain, it better be Glint Junior. If it's you bidding, at least you have a chance to get out. But he loves to give way to the ladies, and always gives in—after he's foreplayed and parlayed their bidding."

"Counselor, the way these things go, you got a bargain . . . only paid ten times what the same scope, unlimited, would have cost down at Barney's Bait and Bullet."

"Tell me about it. I already had to buy her another one because she thinks the auction one is too valuable to use."

"Alcohol and auctions were always a volatile mixture, but adding women gives these sponsors nuclear capability."

"Perfect marketing, though. Both victims believe her presence will hold him down there, sitting on his hands."

"Taking a woman to any auction," the counselor groaned, "is God saying you used to have more money than you thought. The only reason any woman sits on her hands at an auction is to keep them warm and limber for faster bidding."

Beware trips, donating or buying, both. At last count I am owed a trip or two for a year or three by outfitters who, their answering machines tell me, are always unable to come to the phone because they are either digging worms or out on the veldt tracking a wounded wildebeest. On the other hand, one donated day, guided by me on my favorite stream, has been traded by the buyers and traders so often that I have had to employ RCMP missing persons to find out who now has the voucher. Seems the marriage of the original buyer split up, probably over wildlife auctions, and he absconded to Patagonia to fish, while his lovely wife got the voucher back in the settlement. Now I hear she is trying to trade something, anything, for a guide not a shade more steely-eyed than I, but with some hair, for gosh sake.

I bought the last trip I donated when it was going for less than I value the privilege of fishing alone. But the only time survival dictates you must buy is when someone donates a trip for six for a weekend at his cabin on your favorite, "secret" river, lake or stream. Then you hold the voucher and threaten to donate it to the annual outing of the local outlaw bikers if the donor even thinks of doing it again.

There are some other bargains at these affairs, generally in the area of the rare pieces of limited edition original art among umpty-thousand editions of photographic reproductions of a long-gone painting, on which the only original work is the number and autograph of the painter . . . maybe.

So, while everyone is lined up at the bars, wander around, munching on a sandwich from your bag, peering at the prints with the magnifying glass. You may be approached by that tall, thin man, graying, distinguished, wearing dooey cowboy boots and a glint in his eye.

"What you lookin' fer, boy?"

"Dots."

"Say you find some, that good or bad?"

"Good."

If he splats out two four-letter words meaning male bovine organic fertilizer, there is only one reply:

"We need to talk. Hotel bar okay? Where it's quiet?"

One of the worst mistakes I ever made at one of these affairs was when I suddenly decided (I had forgotten the lunch or my personal bar closing or both) to be a Glint myself—a Glint without the gelt.

There was a superb Jack Cowin original print available, an artist's proof, not a dot to be seen, just big red spots on a brown trout fit to blow even a worm-fisherman away. I collect Cowin, but did not have this one. At past auctions I had been horrified by the pittance true original art brought compared to the hyped photographic copies with more dots than the funny page, but autographed by names.

This time, while the auctioneer was trying to shame a bid, any bid, out of the buzzing crowd, something made my hand shoot up and I heard old Magnum Mouth bellow "five hundred dollars," that being about what Cowin original prints were then bringing in Canadian galleries.

Well, that woke up the real Glints. Fortunately my survival instincts returned and drove me, dribbling my blank cheque, to the sidelines. Perhaps I could have bought the print with patient bidding in dribs and dabs. But Trout Unlimited profited immensely. Even Jack Cowin observed a moment of silence out of respect for the buyer when he heard the final price. I experienced the warm glow of the Glints of this world and wonder how I can repeat the experience without going down for the last time during those good cries with my bank manager.

Join them to beat them is how, with an auction sponsored by a coalition of the many worthy groups of which I am a member, but which are too small, individually, to hold their own auctions. Why there's Algophobics Unanimous and Victims Against Solid Water Angling, organizations dedicated to helping their victims combat the addictions of, respectively, moose hunting and ice fishing. Not to mention the self-explanatory North Raven Maniacs, the Sons of Brittanies, the Road Kill Fryers and Tyers and the Black Jack Lubricating and Debating Society and so they go on.

With the thousands we would no doubt collect from gala dinner auctions in aid of such worthy causes, we would have a win-win mandate:

a. Counsel victims of chronic wildlife auction syndrome to deal with their guilt if ever they summon the strength either to just say no, or, even to go, but not bid;

b. If we failed in (a), provide sufficient funds so victims can attend auctions, indulge their addiction by bidding in the style of a Glint, without guilt, and thus even feel good—and solvent—about themselves.

Naturally any items purchased would be the property of the coalition to be sold at its next auction. These affairs are inbred anyway. At them you see officials of Trouts swimming with Ducks, Pheasants crowing in harmony with bugling Elks. Everyone is quacking and burbling "what goes around comes around," and "money is made round to go 'round," and other clichés of the rubber Ducks circuit.

Now, where did I put old Glint Junior's card?

25

Hard Water Porn

IN OUR PART OF THE COUNTRY, THE WINTER OF OUR DISCONTENT is usually January and February, when people have had about enough of hard weather. But it can be even worse during those winters when the Chinook blows for weeks on end, conjuring the prolonged and false illusion of spring, driving people crazy. That's when strange things are done. Some of the strangest are done by people who drill holes in ice. On my first ice fishing trip twenty-five years ago, I was an innocent. But my experience and reading has since convinced me that my first trip was typical and at the same time a parody of this sport that dares not say its name.

We had heard a particular lake was hot, so we alternately got stuck and winched for five hours before we finally arrived on the shore of the lake about 3:00 P.M. There were enough of us for each to take a section of our portable shanty, but when we did, we were all blown like so many ungainly iceboats amok all over the surface of the lake, clean to the nearest correction line. By 4:00 P.M. we had assembled ourselves and the shanty and were ready to drill for crushed ice. By 4:30 we were inside, lines down the holes, watching some monstrous brook trout embalmed in ice water, unaware of all our exotic baits: chum and spastic jigging. Soon it became difficult to see anything down there because night was quickly falling. Then the shanty caught on fire.

Now, there is a school of thought that asserts that these frequent fires are cases of arson committed by jealous ice fishermen who do not have shanties. But I distinctly remember we were the only fishermen on that little lake that day. I have a sneaking suspicion most of these fires are cases of arson, but perpetrated by bored members of your own party, if not to inject a little excitement into proceedings, then at least to get people to start thinking about going home. On that first occasion it worked perfectly. After we took the shanty down and stomped out the flames, everyone decided it was too dark to bother assembling it again, so we might as well call it a day. Call it a night, too, midnight, before we finished blowing about the lake in the dark, finding the vehicle, getting stuck, then unstuck by winching, then having a few at the first bar civilization offered to warm us up and calm our nerves.

That was it. I took the pledge and have since broken it only on the average of once a year, when a friend battling cabin fever or Chinook madness needs help, or a hullabaloo of kids insists I go ice fishing. Basically I believed I knew all there was to know, or all that was good for me to know, about an activity that seemed merely a substitute, just something else people have to suffer before the real fishing begins.

In my innocence that is all I thought was wrong with ice fishing until the day I read a Patrick McManus piece describing some shocking practices of ice fishermen. Even more shocking, McManus then confessed that he had become one of them, a twisted, demented addict of this perversion of angling. He may even have done some other bragging.

Stunned, I went to the local Fly Shoppe to obtain some peacock herl to tie flies and prepare myself for fishing in its proper season as done by normal fishermen. Over the years I have lost nearly everything in sporting goods stores, including sanity and solvency, but that was the first time I ever lost my innocence. There were vile and obscene whisperings: "Strubel Lake . . . gotta be there before sunup . . . stay till after dark . . . action like you can't believe . . . wild! . . . gonna camp out on the ice to be where it's at when it happens. . . ."

Surely somebody whispered in jest. Previously I have praised ice fishing as the occupation of the terminally bored to bring their cabin fever to a head and send them into a coma, but I have never said anything bad about it. Never would I have believed it was the perversion to out-sleaze them all. Get up before dawn? To go ice fishing? I sought reassurance in a browse at my bookstore of Andrew Macpherson's *The Canadian Ice Angler's Guide.* Nothing. But perhaps I looked too quickly, as people do when they peek publicly at pornography. If this praise helps sell Andrew's book, so be it.

Certainly I can understand it, not condone it, mind you, if a person with incurable cabin fever or a deadly infection of Chinook-induced positive ions thinks it might help to induce a hypnotic state by watching water freeze. People in great pain are entitled to pursue whatever comfort, however misguided.

But actually to arise from horizontal in a soft, warm bed to go out in the cold dark to drill holes, molest maggots, abuse leeches, chum with korn kernels and fondle marshmallows in dayglow colors and odors? Surely there has to be a provision in the Criminal Code to deal with such deviants.

Ice fishing is a social problem. Some years ago I set up a self-help group, any member of which, tormented by the sordid urge to ice fish, might call another member who will invite him to rush over and get drunk instead. Do-gooders everywhere will be demoralized by how we are rewarded. The pitiful objects of our concern scurry, that's what they do, like baby seals to the ice. Once there, they bundle under blankets, or erect rural slums rivaling the worst on the outskirts of Mexico City. It would torture civilized discourse to speculate how they keep warm under those blankets, but in the smoky dark of those shanties they are free to commit any atrocity their fevered minds can hallucinate. A fellow I know heard from someone who swore there is a rumor going around that there may even be a little drinking done in those ice huts.

While I was mulling all this, I had to deliver an article to Barry Mitchell, publisher of *The Alberta Fishing Guide*, as sober and steady a gent as there is, dedicated, so I thought, to everything in its proper season. For example, his dearly beloved, the editor, Ann, reports that Barry never does anything about next year's *Guide* until the year's deer season has been properly finished. The back door of Barry's 4x4 was open when I pulled up behind it, and there was an ice auger in there.

Barry was displaying all the symptoms: eyeballs spinning and shifty, jaws clenched like he was already munching crushed ice.

"Care to go fishing?" he asked.

"Didn't know anything was open."

"Ice fishing," he whined.

I gave him a look.

"Thought so," he said. "Anyhow, the kids around here insist, and I gotta go."

That's what these icephiles all say: "It's the kids' fault I'm corrupting them."

The whispers suggested there is a doldrum period from 9:00 A.M. to 3:00 P.M. when the trout stop biting, but a person could go perch fishing elsewhere, then rush back for what would be the evening "rise," were it not for all that ice over-head. Can the voice of temperance and sanity be heard to ask: are these maniacs insatiable? Imagine missing happy hour! Of course, some of them probably go both ways while they are committing that evening ice fishing: doing that infernal jiggy jigging with one hand, while having a drink with the other. Come to think of it, many of the ingredients of a cocktail party will already be available: shrimps, moldy cheeses, maybe even stuffed olives. Eating junk bait like that should not faze people, some of whom I have seen warm up maggots under their lower lips.

Obviously it is time for public relations. From time to time the antihunters mount a campaign against what they perceive to be the reason men hunt: to prove their manhood. They are absolutely right, of course, as any real hunter knows, including the thousands of women who love to hunt.

So the antis run ads featuring some famous, beautiful woman, lips glistening, mouth a-pucker like an ice-fished whitefish kissing the world good-bye in a snowbank, beckoning all male (we hope) hunters to prove their manhood another way. No matter that the pleasure of that other proof is momentary, the position ridiculous and the cost infinite, as Chesterfield wrote, nor that the rest is boredom and bad temper fit to drive a person to diversions like . . . well . . . ice fishing. The campaign has worked to an extent, as the army of liberated men attests that does its hunting of a Saturday morning by pushing a supermarket cart as Mother scouts ahead for new bargains. Perhaps a poster could do something to combat the disease of ice fishing.

How about a gorgeous woman come-hithering and rampant over a glazing ice hole, the whole scene bulls-eyed in the now familiar and forbidding red circle and slash? No word of print needed, which is good; one sometimes wonders if ice fishermen can read, judging by the number of them that ignore thin ice warnings each year, thus causing Search and Rescue to go ice fishing for frozen bodies and rusted metal.

But no, it will not work. If I know ice fishermen, they will just take Mother, or the live-out live-in, whoever it is cranks their auger, with them when they go to camp on the ice, so they can be up early, open a fresh can of kernels and revel in a little more of that hard-water porn.

No, I will not, like McManus, become one of them just because I can't beat them. I'm immune. Well . . . almost. I went twice last winter. This is not a confession; it's a complaint. You see, there was this rumor, attributed to a usually reliable source, that somebody might actually have caught a fish. . . .

26

The Where-to of How-to

ONE PROBLEM WITH WRITING THE HOW-TO ARTICLE IS THAT you either confuse the beginner by assuming he knows something obvious, or insult the expert by assuming he doesn't know everything. Then there is always the daunting thought that someone might actually do what you tell them. Take this excerpt from the "Getting Started" series in *Sports Afield*, this one on upland bird hunting in the October 1985 issue, where author Lionel Atwill assumes all the risks:

"More often than not the gun you can shoot is the gun that fits you—that is, the gun that shoots where you look.

"You can easily test for this. Tack a newspaper page onto the side of the garage and pin a playing card in the middle. Back off twenty yards, hold the gun at high port, concentrate on the card, then pull up the gun and without looking at barrel, rib or front bead and without consciously forming a sight picture, fire. If the card is in the middle of the pattern, your gun fits. The shot imbedded in the garage is a badge of your bird-hunting prowess. If the gun shoots awry, consult a good smith. The stock can be altered, which is always easier and less expensive than buying a new gun, which may not fit, either. Once you have a gun that fits, practice as often as you can."

The Where-to of How-to

Dear Mr. Atwill:

The how-to is adequate, but the where-to may be a little subtle.

You mention earlier in your article about good bird hunters just asking farmers point-blank: "Any birds around here?" Your optimism on the response this question will elicit is touching, but around here they generally respond: "Them birds is spoke fer." Have you ever asked a landowner if he'd mind if you touched a round or two off at his biffy twice-removed, let alone at his barn, silo, granary or garage, to see if your shotgun was shooting where you look? Where I was looking next was out the gate; I might say that the language that invited me to look there did not make me anticipate with pleasure the trip to where else the landowner suggested I could go.

On reviewing your article, I perceived that I had failed to appreciate the subtleties of literary ambiguity. "Tack a newspaper page onto the side of the garage and pin a playing card in the middle," you advise. What page, of what newspaper? Which card? Though I jest on these details, you must admit that "the garage" is at least open to the interpretation that someone else's garage, rather than your own, is prescribed. Only the niggling grammarian would say "preferable."

Not to put too fine a point on it, I tacked the letters page from a week-old, unread Sunday Times to the side of my garage up here in Hyannis, and to that I affixed the joker from a new deck. Do you think my mistake was carrying my new Purdey around the yard with me while I was making my preparations? As you can imagine, antigun nuts abound here, but you like to think people in a neighborhood like this tend a little more than elsewhere to their own affairs. Perhaps I do them an injustice. Herself, who has not been herself lately, may have feared I intended one of us some harm although we had just finished what I recall as a pleasant little reconciliation lunch and two bottles of an excellent Pouilly Fuisse.

But you know, Mr. Atwill, a Purdey practically carries itself. Despite the fact that I waited thirty months for it and paid £ 15,000, not counting the cost of three trips to "merry olde" for fittings, you are absolutely right: I did wonder whether my new gun "shoots where I look," so I paced off the twenty yards; then I starboarded arms (we right-handed readers wonder if you have a bias to the left). Anyway, dutifully oblivious to all the things you advise ignoring, I touched off the right barrel in the general direction of my garage, if not exactly dead on the joker.

"Drop it and freeze!" came the command over a bullhorn before the echo of my shot died away.

For a moment I did congeal in the red and blue light show and the hooting and howling of sirens. Then I panicked, but Purdey and I did make the safety of the garage. Six vehicles it accommodates, but no phone! Fortunately I responded to the persistent ringing of the one upstairs in the chauffeur's quarters. The demands were nonnegotiable: I had five minutes to throw out my iron and come out with my hands on my head, or the tear gas, then the swat team were coming in.

Naturally I complied forthwith. Now I am under indictment, on bail and ordered to have no resort to firearms or alcoholic beverages until these matters are dealt with in the courts. My attorney tells me that if the courts proceed with their customary dispatch, I should miss only the next five upland seasons, by which time my liver should be as soft as angel food. I am sorry, Mr. Atwill, the court order ties me up so tightly I am forbidden even to point and dry fire my finger, let alone "practice as often as you can," as you so wisely advise, assuming, of course, you do not mean shooting again at the garage.

But it is unlike me to be bitter. "If the gun shoots awry, consult a good smith. The stock can be altered. . . ." Do you mean a blacksmith? Where do you find one of those in these days of disposable everything? They don't make even Purdeys like they used to. Or have you never seen one after it has been thrown out a second floor window onto Italian marble flagstones?

"The shot imbedded in the garage is a badge of your bird hunting prowess. . . ." A sixteen square-foot section of the wall of our garage is Exhibit B for identification in The State vs. Truehart. That is actually what has upset Herself more than anything else. She is fond of quoting the decorator who "did" the garage and house in aged cedar shakes: "Madame, thith ith not carpentry, it'th thculpture." Besides, my wife did not want a window in the garage precisely there.

Ironic that: one of the reasons those farmers won't let you shoot even at their oldest barns and granaries is because of the big money they make from decorators for those gray old boards—and the cheesier with wormholes, the better.

There is one ray of hope. Exhibit A for identification, the Purdey, even in its lamentable condition, has disappeared. Questions of who will watch the watchmen aside, those of us committed to the right of free men to keep and bear arms are comforted to know that there are still persons in police departments who really do know and cherish fine guns.

Should Exhibit A turn up, the trial will proceed. In that eventuality, my attorney says, we will have to produce expert evidence before any jury, properly instructed, will believe that what I was doing and where I was doing it was the innocent act of a sane man, let alone that it was done at the urging of an expert writing in the so-called "hook and bullet" press. Mr. Atwill, I have always presumed you were at least an expert, and humbly request your reply to three questions:

1. *Do you think Exhibit A, if it is ever recovered, will shoot where I am looking now?*
2. *Would the test have worked better with the ace of spades pinned to an old op-ed page from* Newsday?
3. *Will you appear voluntarily, or will we have to subpoena you?*

Yours truly,

Allwood Q. Truehart III

27

Hunting the Moggie

IT FINALLY PENETRATED MY PSYCHE THAT THE LATE TWENTIETH century is the age of individual initiative in game management. Budgets are tight, staff is shrunk. Fish and Wildlife divisions will use ideas, whatever their source, as long as they are free. If Joe Schlump, the garbageman out there at Pothole, wants a season shortened and writes one letter to the Minister, then Lo! it shall come to pass.

So, as a public service, I suggested a game-management solution to a pressing social problem. This was the only time I ever tried such a thing, and I did it through the medium of my weekly outdoors column, rather than through a private letter to those in a position to take action. Here is what I wrote:

Quietly a handful of progressive Alberta cities is preparing a cat control bylaw for fall passage.

Well, it is about time! Any day now we were going to be treated to the spectacle of some dog owner charged with harboring a wayward dog, arguing that the local dog bylaw discriminated against dog owners, not to mention dogs.

Cat lovers have always taken the lofty and superior position that cats are different, that you cannot confine them. Now that we have proclaimed fundamental rights and freedoms, that old argument leaks worse than it ever did.

Under the Charter of Rights and Freedoms, nobody or nothing is permitted to be different anymore: gays equal straights, black is white, man is woman, young is old, and so it goes. Now the councils of a couple of our more progressive cities have seen the future and are about to decree that cats are dogs.

One city bylaw officer saw only one problem: the bylaw would be expensive to enforce because it is difficult to catch the agile felines. What nonsense. The general and political columnists have all had a kick at the cat, now allow an outdoors columnist to make a modest proposal. . . .

First you have the provincial government take the domestic cat off the fur-bearing predator—or varmint—list and declare it a big game animal. Declaring the cougar a big game animal a few years back was the best thing that ever happened to the species because then people got interested in the cougar and provided the money to study and manage it.

The cougar is nothing but an overgrown sack of domestic cats anyway, albeit scarce enough that we hunt it only in January.

Given the change in status, we could declare seasons on domestic cats (I would suggest year-round) and limits (would none be too restrictive?)

Hard to catch? Reduce the age limit for a domestic cat license and turn loose the seethings of small boys out there with not enough to do. This brings back tradition. My father told me there was only one thing he could hunt when he grew up in the back alleys of London: "moggies," alley cats. Much more of this talk of privatization of wild game in North America and we will all have progressed back to where there is nothing left to hunt but moggies. But back then it always bothered me that the old man never mentioned what you did with a moggie once you caught him. . . .

Cougars can be hunted only with dogs. It is the nature of all cats to tree quickly when pursued by a dog. Then they can be caught. With the small cats, all you need is a ladder and a landing net.

Which reminds me that you can also fish for cats, as anyone discovers who leaves a fly rod leaning around with a fly dangling loose where cats are also, as usual, loose. Any fly will do, but the Deer Hair

Mouse is best, tied on a #4 hook and using a 1x leader. Dressing the fly with oil of catnip helps the float—cats will walk on air to get it. Be sure to have lots of backing, because even just an average cat can take a lot of line on that first run. But we digress. . . .

Cats hold well for a pointing dog. We once timed my old Brittany, Quince, at one hour, thirteen minutes, holding a one-eyed Persian in the peonies.

Scads of small boys and their dads have good dogs that need work on game, and cats are the natural game of all dogs. Sell a domestic cat license. Then you will have the money to study why people keep cats in the first place, why they let them run and breed at large and how their numbers can be kept within the carrying capacity of their range.

If the sport hunters cannot do the job, then the public control officers will have to mop up, and they have a dog pile to pick from down at the pound, some of the components of which have formerly earned fast livings chasing fat cats.

That's what you can do with the dogs in the pound, but what do you do with the moggies—er—cats? Many will be recycled after pound fees and fines are paid, of course, to their nonconfining, freedom-loving owners. But what of the rest?

Well, I can tell you that many members of the Outdoor Writers of Canada ate cougar for the first time at their annual conference early in July in Courtenay, and many are still raving about how good it was. . . .

So I wrote, and the first manifestation of reader response was a copy of the column, slashed from one of the newspapers in which it appeared, with "Sick, Sick" scrawled on it in black laundry marker. Now that causes compassion to well up within me. If the sender will only supply the return address he forgot on his envelope, I will see that he gets proper professional help.

Then the scat really hit the fan, in a manner of speaking. The Sierra Club continued its policy of taking its cause to the back alleys of the world. "The alley cat population explosion is our fault," thundered their communiqué. "We have expanded the carrying capacity of their range by putting our garbage up in green plastic bags instead of good galvanized iron with a lid."

The Wilderness Society also pleaded *mea culpa*, saying that human foibles have resulted in low numbers of the natural controls on cats—dogs and rocking chairs are scarcely to be found at large any more—and if man upsets the balance of nature, killing the excess result is not the answer.

Killing is never the answer, the naturalists opined, forgetting I was once one of them and had to quit because I could not stand the violence and ingenuity with which they bring death to anything that bothers their beloved songbirds—sparrows, starlings, magpies, squirrels and, yes, cats. Perhaps we could bell the little things, a few of the naturalists sweetly suggested, forgetting that the majority of people are concerned with what it is loose cats do with their other end and on whose property they do it.

The Humane Society took a strong moral view. Killing is wrong. Period. Unless, of course, it is done by them, their way, and not by anyone else in any way from which any peripheral good could be said to result whatever; i.e., no hunting season whatever.

When the trend was well developed, we even heard from Farley Mowat. He tended to blame the white man, everywhere, especially white Anglo-Saxon Protestants not wearing kilts. If it were not for us, went Mowat's thesis, the word *moggie* would be as unknown on the continent as the hunting of them. Amen, I say, and we probably would not even have the moggie here to boot. The natives would never have messed with anything as fundamentally useless as the domestic cat.

Bridgit Bardot turned up in a Lynx coat and fondling a Siamese kitten that is as far from a North American back alley as I am from the Left Bank. She seemed to be telling us what real men do instead of hunting moggies. My friend Griz said this last hunting season that real men don't peel their kielbasa.

Meanwhile, the representative organization of the real hunting men was saying absolutely nothing. No doubt the Fish and Game Association was occupied more with how to pay for its new hideout than it was with providing a glorious new sporting opportunity for its members and, incidentally, helping society mop up one of its problems at the same time.

Not surprisingly, the bulk of the calls, cards, letters and public pronouncements came from the unrepentant cat lovers themselves. What was startling was the uniform tone of their protests. I lacked compassion and understanding, and should have been the first to see that the solution to the problem lies in all that is explicit and implied in one simple word: neutering.

Well, I be dog if the cat lovers have not hit on it right on, first crack, and I'll be the first to doff the old hunting hat to them! Why, do you realize that if we just got on with a mandatory neutering program right now, that in only a nongeneration or two cat lovers would be extinct in this country?

28

Reasonable Moose vs. Moron in a Hurry

THERE WAS ONCE A GROUP OF LAWYERS WHO ANNUALLY WENT on an old-time moose hunt. Then, one year, one of the damn fools up and shot a moose.

Out there knee-deep in half-frozen muskeg, cutting and heaving, 500 meters beyond the reach of all the winch line, haywire, rope, binder twine, even dental floss in camp, the counselor with the water-logged artificial leg eventually cast his weary eyes to the heavens and whined:

"God, is there no such thing as a reasonable moose?"

Even though these lads never have gone moose hunting again, a serious question deserves a serious answer. So we will do what lawyers do when all else fails: look up some law and prepare a brief.

Strangely the legal texts do not define *moose*, so we will have to make one up: a moose is a mule designed by a government task force.

In defining *reasonable*, even the venerable *Stroud's Judicial Dictionary* descends to humor: "It would be unreasonable to expect an exact definition of the word *reasonable*."

Where we really get some action in the musty tomes is with the ancient doctrine of the "reasonable man," whose behavior, according to *Black's Law Dictionary*, we must emulate, in all the circumstances, including the foreseeability of harm to one such as the plaintiff, if we hope "to avoid liability for negligence." No better illustration of the doctrine of the reasonable man exists than in the fictitious case (the only fictitious case in this brief) of *Fardell vs. Potts* by British humorist and barrister A.P. Herbert:

"He is one who invariably looks where he is going, and is careful to examine the immediate foreground before he executes a leap or bound; who neither star-gazes nor is lost in meditation when approaching . . . the margin of a dock; (who) will inform himself of the history and habits of a dog before administering a caress . . . who never from one year's end to another makes an excessive demand upon his wife, his neighbors, his servants, his ox, or his ass . . . who never swears, gambles, or loses his temper; who uses nothing except in moderation . . . this excellent but odious character stands like a monument in our Courts of Justice, vainly appealing to his fellow-citizens to order their lives after his own example."

In other words, the reasonable man is completely unlike your hunting and fishing buddy or mine. Or wife, for that matter. As the fictitious judge holds at the end of Fardell: "I find that at Common Law a reasonable woman does not exist." In these days of political correctness, no real judge could get away with that.

It was only a matter of time until the courts had to create another fictitious being to recognize the steady evolution of modern man away from reason. Appropriately the birth took place in England, origin of the common law, in the 1979 case where *The Morning Star*, a small, staid communist newspaper, was suing Express Newspapers to stop them from naming their new, sensationally headlined tabloid, featuring bare breasts, *The Daily Star*.

Mr. Justice Foster created the new being in one sentence: "I for myself would find that the two papers are so different in every way that only a moron in a hurry would be misled."

Since then, in another case or two involving confusion of this with that, the English courts have breathed enough additional life into this fictitious creature to elevate the moron in a hurry to the status of a modern legal doctrine, perhaps as an antidote to the insufferable reasonable man. It is only a matter of time until Canadian courts notice, and cases involving fishing and hunting provide particularly fertile territory for this new mutation of Homo sapiens to flourish.

Take the 1962 British Columbia Court of Appeal case of *Regina vs. Weber* as a horrible example. Weber was hunting moose along Crooked River when, about 7:00 A.M., he saw something moving on the river and fired two shots at 365 yards. What he thought was a moose was really a fourteen-foot aluminum boat with outboard on stern and three men in it. His first shot killed one of the men in the boat and wounded another. The second shot missed.

In considerably increasing the jail sentence for criminal negligence, Mr. Justice Robertson applied that word *reasonable* to hunters and hunting: "There are reasonable rules of conduct which most hunters observe and the observance of which can virtually eliminate so-called hunting accidents."

But for the fact he was not to be born yet for five years, His Lordship could have been speaking of the moron in a hurry when he said: "When the respondent saw the boat with three men in it on the water and thought it was a moose he cannot have taken any precaution to confirm his impression before he fired."

Mercifully His Lordship did not also observe that, in most of the civilized world, probably even in British Columbia, it is unlawful to shoot a swimming big-game animal.

More difficult is the 1969 decision of the Saskatchewan Court of Appeal in *Regina vs. McCrea*, regarding a 1965 incident where McCrea, a moose hunter afoot, shot dead a conservation officer who was a passenger riding on a running Bombardier, McCrea then admitted: "I didn't know what I was shooting at when I fired."

With remarkable restraint, Chief Justice Culliton contented himself with quoting the law regarding a variation of the reasonable man: "Under the common law any one carrying such a dangerous weapon as a rifle is under the duty to take such precaution in its use as, in the circumstances would be observed by a reasonably careful man."

Had the creature been born yet, would His Lordship have observed, "Even a moron in a hurry could tell the difference between a moose and a Bombardier?" Probably not in Canada, where our pesky moose is in the habit of imitating semitrailers, even locomotives. In 1940, in Quebec, a moose rammed a ten-ton truck and walked away. The truck had to be towed. In 1950 a moose in northern Ontario charged a train and derailed it. This is true.

All of which makes us think of the dozens of moose— vehicle collisions each year in Canada, and brings me to the case that causes me the greatest problem, the 1988 Manitoba Court of Appeal decision in *Maksymetz vs. Plamondon and Slymak Trucking Ltd.*

This was a civil action for damages arising out of a 1983 head-on collision at night between two tractor-trailer units on a remote section of Highway 39 in northern Manitoba. The road was narrow with snow and ice on the traveled portion. Both drivers were traveling at only ten to fifteen kilometers below the posted limit. There was a DEER CROSSING: NEXT 36 KM sign. Each driver dimmed his lights on seeing the other approach.

Suddenly the defendant noticed a moose on the left side of the highway. The creature gave a couple of jumps, then struck the truck, causing the hood to fly up. The defendant lost control, crossed the center line and collided with the plaintiff.

The court dismissed the Plaintiff's claim. Speaking for the majority, Chief Justice Monnin in essence said that a reasonable man traveling with dimmed headlights would not reduce his speed much below the posted limit simply because of the threat of the sudden appearance of a moose, especially on a highway in a remote area of the province.

Strange. Thousands of Canadian moose hunters would have thought a remote area of Manitoba would be just the place to encounter a moose, and would have been all eyes and in road-huntin' gear for that entire thirty-six kilometers.

But there is worse in the words of His Lordship: "The entire episode was an accident caused by a wayward moose running across the path of his vehicle. . . . Had he reduced (his speed) considerably, would the moose have also reduced his speed and not traveled in the same direction or suddenly jumped in front of defendant's vehicle? . . . The action of the moose was the sole cause of the accident and could be termed an act of God."

Manitoba's highest court seemed to be asking, "Why can't a moose be more like a reasonable man and not a moron in a hurry?" It seemed to me that in blaming the moose or God for the accident, the court was either holding the moose to the standard of the reasonable man or an unreasonable God. It all disturbed me so much I caught a severe dose of writer's block and could not go on with the brief.

Generally I do not show anyone my stuff until it is sent to the editor, but I thought the curious blend of insanity and horse sense of my friend Griz might help. Griz read the brief thus far and nearly wore his finger to the first knuckle on the Maksymetz case.

"Aww . . . right!" Griz exclaimed. "God's out of her; He's never in a rush. So who's the moron in a hurry here—the drivers, the moose or the judges who decided this mess?"

"Uh, Griz, judges can blame God for anything they can't understand, but you can only say something like that about a judge if you first say 'With the greatest of respect, M'Lord.' But what is a reasonable moose?"

"Piece a cake," Griz said. "Trouble with them lawyers up to their tail pipes in that swamp suckin' slough water . . . trouble with all you lawyers is you can't see dam for diversion. . . ."

"Definition, Griz, the definition."

"Got your pencil? Your one and only reasonable moose," Griz dictated, "is one that, dead or alive, comes to a full stop, smack dab in the borrow pit. . . . Now, do I get to say I rest my case?"

29

Stalking the Wild Barberian (Or the Fifteen Loonie Misunderstanding)

THE WORST THING THAT CAN HAPPEN TO A SPORTING GENT IS to lose an old-fashioned, steady-to-wing-and-shot outdoors barber. The second worst is to lose a wife, which is exactly what happened to my Constant Barber, who staunchly resisted changing his last name to "Stylist."

Constant would not allow a blowdryer on premises famous for organic hot air, nor permit much idle chitchat of sex, politics, religion and other such trash. No, Anglish and Huntarian only were spoken in his shop, where seldom was heard a discouraging word, except Constant's own familiar refrain about his tormentors in the Fish and Wildlife division:

"Them dirty, rotten, trough-sloppin' swine!"

Constant was also a competent, careful and caring five-buck barber with the steely eye of the guide and outfitter.

"Been coyote huntin', eh?"

"How do you know?"

"Got you a little mange up here. No sweat; we'll do you the sheep-dip."

For Constant, the second worse thing and his personal first worst—new regulations ended his beloved guiding and outfitting—hit him all at once. Depressed, he planned escaping to a whaler in the Keys with a gorgeous first mate to replace his second worse thing, pausing only long enough to empty the till and utter the refrain one last time:

"Them dirty, rotten, trough-sloppin' swine!"

That left his customers hunting a throwback haircutter, about as rare anymore as finding your hairy Sasquatch within range of a loaded camera—or rifle.

A time or two I thought I had the place, but a female stylist always turned up. Ever tried serious talk in mixed company? This is not sexist. Women without end, and even some with ends that never end, can tolerate male hairdressers, but claim they hate having male customers present. They mention that some things are secret, and is nothing sacred?

A cabin-fevered friend, high-centered between fishing and hunting, gave me an idea when he said he was so starved for excitement he guessed he'd go to Pothole and watch haircuts. So I traveled the whole civilized world within a radius of 100 kilometers, chasing even faded rumors of fresh paint on barber poles. The best I found were escapees of prison barber schools who called themselves stylists and charged eight to twenty dollars per corner.

I stalked the impossible dream of the barbershop of my youth: the incense of talcum and the Eau de Portugal we called stinkum, the click of snooker balls through the open door to the poolroom, the quiet barbershop harmony of male voices trading truths of the pheasant season and swapping lies on "how's the fishing?" There were magic things there for a small boy who kept his ears open and his mouth shut, and who didn't squirm.

Dead silences always immediately met any woman who blundered over the threshold, but particularly thundering was the black hole created the day my Mom blew through the door, dragging me by the ear, hollering: "Who sheared this lamb?" The culprit, Herb, who had been dozing in his chair, apparently with one eye open, like a dog buzzed by flies, lurched bolt upright, then fled, staggering, to the poolroom.

At noon Mom had handed me two bits to get my hair cut after school, automatically adding a third bit: "And no, you cannot have a brush cut." Slim, who owned two fine setters, and Alf, the world's greatest goose hunter, were working heads, so I drew Herb who, by 4:30 P.M. most days, was tipsy from cutting out between cuts to the hotel bar. He steadied himself with his hand flat on the top of my head, occasionally snipping at what hair sprang up between his fingers.

Slim did the only salvage job possible on the hairy handprint, winking at me from time to time in the mirror whenever my dormant volcano of a mother was not looking. I concentrated on not grinning like a kid who was getting his first brush cut.

But from East Alkali to Fort Kindling in the west, this modern civilization we are building has destroyed every last neat place like that barbershop of my youth. What we have now, everywhere, are stylists and designers, male and female, in salons and studios, where all you hear is a discouraging word: hair, hair, hair. I was torn between having what was left of mine shaved off, or going for the mountain man look, where you just let 'er ee—rode from dragging in the dirt.

"Come on," my friend Griz said, "you always say, 'You ain't tried it, don't knock it.' Besides, getting your hair cut by a woman is a sensuous experience."

"Yeah, tell it to Samson. It's in the Bible," I explained.

But I decided to try one of these Unisex places even though Griz warned me that a haircut, straight up, would be fifteen bucks. "Worth every dime and your time," Griz said, and patted my bald dome.

The reception area had no fish or game mounts on the wall, no old hook and bullet magazines on the coffee table, not even any live bait for sale. What reading there was were *Elle* and *Vogue*, junk like that, and the only bait was canned sheep after-birth, guaranteed to grow hair on ceramic tile. They wash hair, dye and burn it in these places, so the smell is outdoorsy: a mixture of wet dog, singed duck and turpentined cat. Unisex? Out there in the salon multisex stylists posed and made faces in mirrors as they danced around their victims.

"Hi, I'm Herbena, but you can call me Herb. I'll be your stylist today."

Great start. Bouncy little thing: if I read the two buttons on her sweatshirt correctly, she was clearly a stylist of the female persuasion. Now, I've shot too much skeet without muffs in my day, and between that and the flushed-in rock music, the yackity-yack of hair talk, the clickity-click of scissors and the hum of the blowdryers, I may not have heard this conversation right. Besides, my on-side ear kept getting plugged with one of those buttons as that poor little thing had to go up on tippy toes just to reach over the ridge and brush out the south side of my clearing.

"Not much up there worth talking about," I said.

"Just a solar collector for a sex machine, is all," she giggled.

"Oh, are you into environmentalism?"

"The only 'isms' I don't do are your saddy and your masochism, etcetera and vice versa."

"How about wildlife?"

"Puh . . . leeze. Love the wild, hold the beastie. That isn't even an 'ism.' But don't you worry, Honey, I'm into the outdoors life . . . if there's a satin . . . I mean . . . you know . . . eiderdown?"

"Yeah, I went two weeks once with my three-star bag—scored for thirty below."

"Outta sight! But, with your modern woman, you'll have to get rid of macho talk like 'bag' and 'score.'"

That's the whole load, as best I can recall. My head's a double parking proposition, a snip and a shine.

"Just call me any time, okay?" she said, after slipping me her card and hugging me on with my coat.

"Okay, Herb, but . . . well . . . I don't know how to say this, but . . ."

"Oh you! You can tell me anything, anything."

"Okay . . . It's just that I'd kinda like it if you would holler something out every once in a while."

"Far out! Your typical screamer bit . . . holler what?"

"Listen carefully and repeat after me: 'Them dirty, rotten, trough sloppin' . . .'"

30

Advanced Tie Flying

No sooner had my pupils adjusted to the gloom of Blackout's Bar 'n' Cue when I spotted one of them, Jason, waving me over. It was that time of a Canadian winter when it is too early for fishing and too late for suicide, when many outdoorspersons think a drink or several might help. Jason, too, was gloomy. He sagged and sighed like a foul-hooked belly boat.

"There's no way out," he groaned. "I've just gotta take up fly tying."

"Whatever the hell for?" I asked.

"I just can't afford store-boughts any more."

I recovered consciousness with Jason pounding me on the back. Almost drowning in Blackout's draft is a fate worse than death, but a laugh like that was worth it.

"Its not funny," Jason said. "This year's order to Dan Bailey's took all my tax refund, and my spousal facsimile ain't functioning as such nor even communicating much."

"Jason . . . Jason my young friend," I said, "the only hobbies that cost more and pay less than fly tying are revenge and adultery, which may be a distinction without a difference, when you get right down to it."

"Come on," Jason said, "you do it—tie flies, I mean."

186

"No way are you going to believe me, but would you believe him?" I asked, pointing at a nearby table.

"Who he?"

"Dibbley Bobbin," I said.

"Not the living legend of fly tying?"

"As he lives and breathes."

"What's he doing?"

The gangly gent had his necktie around his right wrist, using it like a rifle sling to steady his aim and winch his left hand with a glass of dark amber fluid toward his mouth.

"C'mon, we'll ask him."

I introduced Jason, then asked Dib what was it with the sling and sip.

"Tie flying this drink . . . or trying to hang myself from it?" Dib's eyes swam behind his thick glasses like raw oysters in a crystal fish-cocktail dish. "Naw, I lie. It's one a them Catch 22s. I just ain't steady enough to take my medicine until I get the first dose down."

"What's doing this to you, Dib?" I asked.

"Well, I don't like to think it's the medicine, so I guess I'm a cementhead from inhalin' head cement fumes or maybe it's poisonin' from all that lead wire in my wet fly patterns."

"Why don't you just ask for a straw?" Kevin asked.

"Real men don't use straws, son. Can't get her down fast enough that way."

"Jason here's thinking of taking up fly tying because tailor-mades have got too expensive," I said.

"Anyone who thinks they can save money tyin' flies is one hackle short of a neck," Dib pronounced.

"What?" from Jason.

"One BB shy of a full load."

"Then how come you turned pro?" Jason asked.

"Fate. There I was gettin' nowhere, like anyone else. Tyin'

up my year's supply whilst watchin' instant replays until the Stanley Cup play-offs petered out, or until I could puke, whichever came first. It takes long suffering to get addicted to any truly disgustin' vice. Oh, I sold a few: the ones that looked like owl pellets, them was your dry flies. Look like coyote dung? Them was the wets. Then along came the catch-and-release places and the bait bans, and my kinda flies was in with the new, instant fly-fisherpersons, all of which believe if it ain't meat, the fish won't eat."

"The Chinatown Dumpster," Jason chanted reverently, "the Wapiti Gutpile, the Green Oozy Booger, the Hot-wired Whole Squirrel Hide, the Hacked-off Liver Leech. . . ."

"Yup, my masterpiece. Then came the video. . . ."

"Roadkill from Roadkill: Tying Killing Flies from Flattened Fauna," Jason said.

"You got it," Dib said. "Suddenly I'm a star."

"I've always wondered . . ." Jason started.

". . . how many flies can a pro tie per hour, am I right? Like askin' a hooker how she got started or a man how's his sex life, eh? Or, worse, how many miles per gallon he gets from his rig or how many cows he owns?"

"I'm sorry, I'm sorry."

"No problem, kid. It ain't that it's rude, which it is; it's just that them kind of questions plain invites a man to lie," Dib said. "But I am going to give you the gospel. The answer is zero, nada, zilch flies per hour. Hell, I've arrived. You buy my patterns anymore, and they been tied under license, offshore by human robots in Kenya. Now they pay me not to tie, and the more I don't tie, the more they pay me and vicey versey. I may be the highest paid professional nonfly-tier in North America. . . . But let's get back to economic analysis. How much this latest order set you back, son?"

"Well," said Jason, "the start is $1.85 US a pop. Factor in

monetary exchange, G.S.T., customs duty and their $5.00 handling, postage, more handling and insurance . . . I figure pretty close to $3.00 Canadian a fly."

"Such a deal! You're laughin' all the way to the bank! How many you order?"

"Ten dozen."

"Three hundred and sixty loons for the year's supply? Looka here. Just start with the vice, the first thing you gotta have to catch the vice. Last superduper, tie-by-its-ownself machine I saw in a walnut coffin lined with red velvet was $550. Give her a flip and she spun on to eternity or, if that's too short, until you got the mortgage paid off on her. And backlashes? Don't get me started. High-tech junk. Every tier I know has three or four of the latest wonders in storage until he gets around to old faithful, the Thompson A. Figure between a grand and two into your overhead, unless you can sell the stored junk vices to another sucker.

"Add in $1,000 or so for every other fad in tools. Then, for you, the overhead won't be underfoot like it was for me. Naw, roadkill won't be good enough for you, even if you did have the nose and stomach for it. You'll want your premium hooks, the hackle necks from roosters better bred than you are, so as you need a vault to deter thieves and protect against serving gourmet meals to moths. You won't buy bulk like the pro does. You'll be at the mercy of the splitters and dividers that corner markets and cause disasters like the Phentex Famine of '85 and the Pliobond Panic of '89. But all that's nothin'. The worst two parts of a amateur's overhead is to come. . . . What's your day job, Jason?"

"Like Bob . . . I'm a lawyer."

"Okay. Hunnerd and fifty per hour, right? Fifty percent overhead, if you're lucky, am I right again? Seventy-five an hour left for you, fifty after tax. Best you'll ever do is ten flies per hour. There's five bucks each overhead for you before you even tie fly one. A pro ain't got that because he's got no day job. Why don't you just mouthpiece a extry seven, eight hours. . . . Buy your ten dozen and have a few bucks left over to buy me another shot or three of this here medicine."

I waved in the waitress.

"But that ain't even the worst. Pros play by hookers' rules."

"Huh?"

"Pros don't give no freebies . . . Wait . . . You'll get the point, Jason, after I do a little cross-examination. How many flies you tie last year, Bob?"

"Maybe twenty-five dozen."

"How many you have left when you hung her up for the season?"

"Maybe two, three dozen."

"How many you fish yourself?"

"Ten dozen, max."

"Sell any?"

"Please! I'd never do it for money."

"Obviously. So, where's the gone gross, the missing twelve dozen?"

"Well, son John and nephew Kurt look at my fly boxes occasionally, then there's several of my buddies say they like to admire the display. Suddenly they are gone."

"Don't matter anyhow," Dib said. "Half your production's gone to fly box browsin' and boostin', what I call finanglin'. You've just doubled the price. We're closin' in here fast, boys, on ten to fifteen dollars per fly."

"But you've got to give a discount," I said, "for the entertainment value of the great stories the fly finanglers tell."

"Now ain't that the truth," Dib said. "'The old woman don't like the mess,' or 'My daughter's allergic to the *cul de canard* feathers' (that's duck's arse, par'n my English)."

"Or," I interrupted, "there's always the likes of Doc Moller, a practicing root canal specialist, who claims his fingers are too stiff to tie flies."

"Or you, and especially even me, Bob, claiming the eyes ain't good enough any more to tie smaller than 16s, but they're still good enough see finangled 22s floating out at the end of a long cast in a light chop on a dull day."

"But . . . but," Jason spluttered. "What about the challenge, the accomplishment, the satisfaction of catching fish on a perfect fly tied by yourself, using nothing but the finest materials."

"You ever catch any fish at all on them roadkill patterns a mine?"

"Hundreds, maybe even thousands," Jason said.

"I rest my case. Fortunately trouts' brains is just a goose blivet smaller than a fly tier's," Dib said, and turned to flag in one for the roadkill.

Suddenly a great sob came from Jason. His eyes were streaming. His upper lip quivered like a Hacked-off Liver Leech, as though in fear of the natural Green Oozy Booger poised like a python above it.

"B . . . B . . . Bob," Jason blubbered, "n . . . nobody can t . . . tie Le T . . . Tort (hic) H . . . H . . . Hoppers that f . . . float flat l . . . like yours. How a . . . a . . . b . . . out . . . ?

"A perfect finangling finesse. This kid's a natural," Dib said, retying his cravat with his one steady hand, while sipping a shot offhand with the other. "Only one lesson and already the moves of a pro."

About the Author

Bob Scammell has been fishing and hunting for more than forty years and writing about the sports for more than twenty years in an award-winning weekly outdoors column in various Alberta newspapers. He also is a frequent contributor to fishing magazines throughout the West. His first book, *The Outside Story*, was selected the outstanding outdoors book of the year in 1983 by the Outdoor Writers of Canada. He also is the author of *The Phenological Fly: A Method for Meeting and Matching the Super Hatches of the West*. Bob Scammell has served as President of the Alberta Fish and Game Association and as a Director of the Canadian Wildlife Federation.